Terrorists and Terrorism in the Contemporary World

David J. Whittaker

Routledge
Taylor & Francis Group

LONDON AND NEW YORK

D0003838

First published 2004
by Routledge
11 New Fetter Lane, London EC4P 4EE

Simultaneously published in the USA and Canada
by Routledge
29 West 35th Street, New York, NY 10001

Routledge is an imprint of the Taylor & Francis Group

© 2004 David J. Whittaker

Typeset in Times by
Florence Production Ltd, Stoodleigh, Devon
Printed and bound in Great Britain by
TJ International Ltd, Padstow, Cornwall

British Library Cataloguing in Publication Data
A catalogue record for this book is available from the
British Library

Library of Congress Cataloging in Publication Data
Whittaker, David J., 1925–
   Terrorists and terrorism in the contemporary world /
   David J. Whittaker.
      p. cm. – (The making of the contemporary world)
   1. Terrorism.   2. Terrorists.   I. Title.   II. Series.
   HV6431.W49 2004
   303.6′25–dc22   2003020579

ISBN 0–415–32085–2 (hbk)
ISBN 0–415–32086–0 (pbk)

Terrorists and Terrorism in the Contemporary World

Terrorists and Terrorism in the Contemporary World surveys this topical and complex subject. The book concentrates on the terrorists themselves and their psychology in an historical context.

Focusing on a variety of both prominent and less notorious terrorist groups the author encourages readers to think about the mindset, motivation and tactics of terrorists. He also discusses the lines of thought linking contemporary and leading terrorists of the last 30 years.

David J. Whittaker analyses examples of terrorists working as individuals, such as Timothy McVeigh, and those working in groups, such as al-Qaida, over the last two or three decades. He goes on to discuss the problems of countering these terrorists and possible future forms that terrorism might take.

David J. Whittaker was Lecturer in International Relations at the University of Teesside and is now retired. He is the author of a number of publications including *The Terrorism Reader* (now in its second edition) and several other titles in the Making of the Contemporary World series.

The Making of the Contemporary World
Edited by Eric J. Evans and Ruth Henig

The Making of the Contemporary World series provides challenging interpretations of contemporary issues and debates within strongly defined historical frameworks. The range of the series is global, with each volume drawing together material from a range of disciplines – including economics, politics and sociology. The books in this series present compact, indispensable introductions for students studying the modern world.

Contents

Preface

Contemporary terrorists are rarely out of the news. The word 'terrorism' is on all lips to an extent that would have been intriguing 30 years ago. Everybody uses the term and hardly anybody explains it, apart from discussion in books and certain journals with a limited readership.

This is a book with a difference. Its main purpose is to provide a modestly-sized, readable account of a complex subject about which so many questions are asked. In two respects this book opens up new ground. First, readers are encouraged particularly to think about the psychology of terrorists – their mindset, their motivation and their tactics. Second, there is an attempt to trace 'connections', those lines of thought that appear to link contemporary terrorists with some of the thinking trailblazers of the last two or three decades. Much of what contemporary terrorists set out to do is fully understandable only if we take into account some of the thinking and persuasions of earlier years. There follows a description of selected terrorist groups and profiles of three well-known terrorists. Other chapters discuss terrorists and the media, ethical and moral aspects of terrorism, possible future forms of terrorism, and the principles, practice and programmes of counter-terrorism. Finally, in Chapter 11, there is both a résumé of the author's main arguments and a section suggesting a list of topics which should provide scope for reflection, discussion and further enquiry.

A book such as this owes a great deal to sharing the thoughts of others in print, correspondence and conversation. I am grateful to Andrzej Krauze for the cartoons, for the ready helpfulness of librarians in the Universities of Bradford, Durham and Teesside and to Adrian Norton. Marianne Whittaker has given invaluable assistance with psychological aspects of terrorism. At Routledge, I am indebted to Alex Ballantine and Gillian Oliver. Jane Thompson has once again done a splendid job in providing a final manuscript.

For any shortcomings or misinterpretations I alone am responsible.

David J. Whittaker
North Yorkshire

Figure 1 Palestinian students pass a painting depicting a suicide bombing during a university exhibition to mark a year of the *intifada*, September 2001.
© Abed Omar Qusini/Reuters

1 Problems in definition

When the dust cleared from New York's Ground Zero in September 2001, understandable feelings of anger and fear blanketed an immediate search for the meaning of it all. Disbelief in the enormity of close on 3,000 dead did not make for rational and dispassionate analysis. It is, perhaps, only later that Americans and everyone else have begun to look critically at the shape of destructive, political behaviour.

There have been agonised questions. Where was the 'threat' coming from? Who was behind an outrage such as this? Could something similar recur? Questions such as these push for clarification and consensus. America's first impulse, a square-jawed determination to 'root out' and 'take out' 'it' and 'them' gave way to steadier resolve to work out who the enemy was, and to survey methodically methods and predictability. The White House had no illusions about a search of this nature. Coming to grips worldwide with a terrorist menace would stretch beyond our lifetime, declared Vice-President Dick Cheney. A strategy of this scale would demand an international coalition, in the view of President George Bush. However, what were we all fighting against?

The wood, the trees and the terrorists

There is a forest of terrorism definitions, very likely more than a hundred printed ones. It is not always easy to make out the acknowledged standing elements, the trees, as it were, but some criteria of terrorism seem agreed:

- it is a premeditated, politically motivated use of violence or its threat to intimidate or coerce a government or the general public;

- it is a strategy of violence designed to achieve desired outcomes by instilling fear and insecurity;
- there is an unlawful use or threat of force through sustained campaigning or sporadic incidents;
- there is calculated use of violence against civilian, non-combatant targets;
- power is intrinsically at the root of political violence – its acquisition, its manipulation and its employment to effect changes;
- revolutionary terrorism aims at bringing about complete change within a state;
- sub-revolutionary strategies aim at political change without collapsing a political system;
- generally, there is clandestine activity which is carefully planned as to goals, means, targets and access;
- goals may be understood generally as political, social, ideological, or religious, otherwise terrorists would be thought of as delinquent criminals;
- terrorism is usually carried out by sub-national groups, occasionally, by dedicated lone individuals;
- maximum publicity is normally an important objective for terrorists;
- zones of action, hitherto a specific country or locality or segment of society, are fast becoming transnational where ramifications frequently go beyond national boundaries.

There is much common ground with these criteria; equally there are differing points of view. Institutional definitions stress illegality of coercion and of offences against property, facilities and infrastructure. In 2001 the United States administration was at pains to highlight its abhorrence of external violence attacking on home turf its cherished symbols of governance and democracy. Academics, psychologists, criminologists and journalists are particularly concerned in their definitions with what they regard as the causes of political activism becoming violent and with terrorist intimidation making for increased public vulnerability.

Perspectives in definition

A glance at the above list shows some disapproval and readiness to judge. It looks as though terrorism as an *ism* is given a meaning which we, as appalled witnesses or readers, consider it deserves. Much of this may depend upon the perspective used. Differences in view might be expected from an *authority* responsible for order and peace, from an *onlooker*, either one who saw things at first hand or following events on radio and television, from a *victim* or relation, and, lastly, from one of the *terrorists* themselves:

- The *authority* must crack down on what it sees as behaviour going beyond the limits of protest and convention. A state's response will be prompt and prescriptive to remove a threat to peace, order and security. This 'no nonsense' view leaves little room for consideration of causes.
- *Onlookers* naturally deplore vicious, lethal, anti-social behaviour. The more conservative media outlets and much anecdote focus on political protest gone mad. Often, behaviour seen as disruptive may be thought malevolent and the term 'terrorism' expanded in meaning to describe a wide range of protest such as 'football hooliganism' or 'lager loutism' or 'conference busting'.
- *Victims*, innocent or targeted, must see the violence involving them with a sense of dramatic finality, for it denies them perhaps life, mobility and health. Where political violence shuts down people's freedom to move where they want (as, for instance, with Palestinians and Israelis), then terrorist operations are an excluding factor violating basic human rights and making large numbers of unfortunate people victims in a real sense.
- *Terrorists* will be branded as destructive maniacs, as evil-minded, as irresponsible wreckers of civilised codes. Whereas the general community may be disposed to consider consequences rather than causes, certainly when they are in a state of shock, most of those who resort to political violence, first of all, disclaim any sweeping label such as 'terrorist', and go on to affirm that they have had little option other than violence to make their case plain, and are generally anxious to voice their own idealistic, even altruistic, goals.

Very clearly the meanings of terms such as 'terrorism' and 'terrorist' are heavily dependent upon the approach and the angle of view of those who would define. Nor can prejudice, even prompt vilification, be ruled out. There is much to be said for the opinion of Professor Richard Falk, of Princeton, speaking to journalists in 1997, that terrorists are often viewed 'through a self-righteous, one-way, moral-legal screen where positive images of Western values stand threatened by unrestricted political violence'.

Distinctions and more distinctions

Words and attitudes wrap around meaning especially when there is some difficulty in distinguishing terrorist from guerrilla from 'freedom fighter'. With these three, there are contrasts in their recourse to violence:

* the *terrorist* targets civilians;
* the *guerrilla* goes for military personnel and facilities;
* the *freedom fighter* conducts a campaign to liberate his people from dictatorial oppression, gross disarmament, or the grip of an occupying power.

The terrorist exploding bombs (perhaps a suicide bomber) in a Tel Aviv shopping mall or in a Moscow theatre is regarded as criminal, regardless of motivation. He or she places no limits on their methods which result in widespread terror and mayhem. Nothing is held to excuse the act and if caught the terrorist is summarily punished. On the other hand, the guerrilla operating in a group to fight a 'people's war' proclaims dedication to a just cause, selecting and hitting what they see as legitimate military targets, as did Fidel Castro in Cuba, the Argentinian Che Guevara and Robin Hood and his Merry Men in medieval England. They may be admired – with a touch of romance and mystique about it. The so-called 'freedom fighter' is devoted to an inescapable struggle, as in Mozambique, Bosnia and Nicaragua.

What distinguishes the terrorist from the others is not the extent of violence: it is the choice of target and mode of activity. Whether guerrilla or freedom fighter, if violence is used against innocent civilians then you are most certainly a terrorist. No end can justify such means. It can happen, of course, that guerrilla bands, making little progress in their fight against a repressive regime, either purposefully harm a number of non-combatants or they are unable to avoid doing so because their operations become threatened by security forces. The Tamil Tigers, fighting savagely in Sri Lanka for their independence, are regarded as terrorists rather than as a liberating force because they destroy villages and assassinate political figureheads. When Chechen 'rebels', fighting for their national autonomy, spring violence upon Moscow, they are hunted as 'terrorists'; if at home in Chechnya they sabotage Russian military bases they are lauded by their fellows as brave patriots. Another example of contradistinction is that of the various Resistance Movements in Occupied Europe during the Second World War. The occupying German Army, on capturing individuals, would show them no mercy and shoot them out of hand as contemptible terrorists. Resistance headquarters, though, gave strict orders to their 'freedom fighters' to avoid civilian loss whenever possible. In any case, some distinguishing descriptions change in time and circumstance. Freedom leaders such as Archbishop Makarios in Cyprus, Jomo Kenyatta in Cyprus, Nelson Mandela in South Africa and Fidel Castro in Cuba were despised and attacked by a beleaguered authority at the outset of their liberation campaigns. Ultimately, they were awarded international honour and a President's chair.

International law and the definition of terrorism

International law confers a duty upon a state to prevent within its borders political terrorist activities directed against any foreign state's independence or territory. These activities will be held to be terrorist if they result in injury, death or destruction within the borders of a sovereign state. This obligation seems based on a definition that is really rather loose. Some of the ways in which terrorism has been codified in various ways by international bodies for many years are these:

- *1937*: the League of Nations drew up a Convention for the Repression of International Terrorism which laid upon signatories the duty neither to encourage nor tolerate any terrorist activity with a political purpose and to do all in its power to prevent and repress it;
- *1949*: the United Nations International Law Commission reaffirmed the above duty in article 4 of a Draft Declaration on the Rights and Duties of States;

- *1971*: the Organisation of American States also reaffirmed the above duty;
- *1972*: the United Nations General Assembly set up a 35-member *Ad Hoc* Committee on Terrorism;
- *1975*: the Helsinki Declaration of the Conference on Security and Cooperation in Europe, signed by 30 European states, the United States, Canada and the Holy See, pledged members 'to refrain from direct or indirect assistance to terrorist activities';
- *1977*: the Council of Europe opened for signature a European Convention on the Suppression of Terrorism;
- *1979*: the United Nations General Assembly adopted an International Convention against the Taking of Hostages;
- *1982*: the Council of Europe adopted a recommendation about International Cooperation in the Prosecution and Punishment of Terrorism;
- *2001–2*: the United Nations opened for signature an International Convention for the Suppression of Terrorism.

Difficulties, though, remain. Short of an acceptable international definition of terrorism, in reality, any state can sign a declaration against terrorism without needing to put obligations into full practice. States party to a Convention tend to define the phenomenon of terrorism in different ways. Terrorist activity within a certain country will be rigorously contained: violent political activities occurring elsewhere may be regarded fatalistically or even ignored. On the other hand, it ought to be possible to secure some fundamental agreement on an outline definition that regards the work of terrorists as intentional use of violence against non-combatant civilians aimed at reaching certain political ends. Brutal attacks of this kind would be considered by all as barbaric and unacceptable. They would have nothing at all to do with conventional war between military forces, where characteristics, principles and limitations are already firmly codified in Geneva and Hague Conventions. They would also be different from guerrilla warfare which, as was pointed out earlier, differs from terrorism in targeting military personnel rather than civilians.

Since New York's traumatic 9/11 there has been a great deal of international effort to put what is understood to be unacceptable terrorism at the very top of the agenda. The United Nations system of specialised agencies and programmes is continually devising a raft of counter-terrorist measures (as we shall see more fully in Chapter 10) to supplement those of the 1960s and 1970s. Now there are 12 anti-terrorism treaties and just as many Conventions compelling all 189 supporting nations to work together against aiding, supporting, harbouring, organising and sponsoring terrorists. As we shall see in Chapter 10, the 15 members of the European Union are putting into force an ambitious anti-terrorist plan of action.

Context as a key to meaning

Martha Crenshaw, an American political scientist, has written in detail about the significance of context in an analysis of terrorism (Crenshaw 1995: 7–24). For her there are few 'neutral terms' in politics. In thinking about terrorism there is a need to understand, as objectively as we can, not only the facts presented by terrorist incidents but also their significance symbolically. There will be a mix of meanings, those intended by the perpetrators of outrage, those given it by witnesses, all too often done so hastily, and the constructions governments and the public place upon them. Crenshaw believes that the task of definition through a study of the historical and political contexts that enclose a scenario involves, in her words, 'transforming "terrorism" into a useful analytical tool rather than a polemical tool' (Crenshaw 1995: 24). Following this train of thought it seems clear that what has happened in Northern Ireland or Sri Lanka or among the Basques will be hard to understand unless the whole picture is examined – without taking sides.

Scrutinising what we can make out as social, political, religious and ideological factors in a context, and the importance, too, of time and place, should altogether help reduce certain hasty and narrow perceptions on these lines:

- premature moral judgement branding certain actions as 'illegitimate' or 'evil';
- over-hasty view of actions as 'unnecessary', 'irresponsible', 'avoidable', 'fanatical';
- blurring distinctions between violent and non-violent tendencies;
- again, a premature prescriptive view which forecloses possibilities of compromise and perhaps eventual settlement;

- rigid attitudes set in such a mould as 'there can never be a deal with terrorists';
- rigidity which fails to discern the importance of message and myth (particularly to those fighting for liberation and those in authority seeking to contain or extinguish it).

One could say that narrowness of perception – not thinking about the context widely enough – led to many difficulties, for instance, for Britain and France in coping with sporadic and sustained violence in their former African and South East Asian colonies after 1945. More than half a century later we can understand how Empires with their backs to the wall pinpointed would-be liberators as destructive 'terrorists'. Nowadays, there is so much comprehensive discussion of terrorism in the press and on television screens that it should not be too formidable a task to lace together what appear to be motivating causes for endemic violence, say, in Northern Ireland, among Palestinians or in Indonesia. Yet, there will always be problems with our readiness to define, to make sense of it all. Crenshaw, once more reflecting on the usefulness, if not the overriding importance, of considering the terrorist-in-context, warns us that if political circumstances urge us towards definition then 'the taboo associated with the word itself is so powerful that different definitions unavoidably produce different political consequences' (Crenshaw 1995: 19).

Widening contexts

Certainly, most political commentators and writers are well aware of the importance of widening contexts as an essential aid to understanding. Two examples may illustrate this point. First, in Northern Ireland, 30 years of armed conflict are presently in a state of suspense balanced on a fragile peace agreement. The whole tragic picture – and conjecture about why terrorists still roam the streets – only makes sense if one takes account of long memories of discrimination, confrontation and struggle reinforced by quasi-religious myths of victimisation and sacrifice. The Irish context stretches over three centuries with elements of English colonial dominance, politico-military fighting between extremists on rival flanks, and a continuing toe-to-toe battle for civil rights. Those who resorted to terrorism inescapably were honoured as patriots. What alternative could there possibly be?

Intolerance, suspicion and violent outbursts still play a central role in prising Catholic and Protestant apart and in decelerating the momentum of the peace process. Ulster's continuing experience puts a ragged edge on definition when it throws up a troubling question: has terrorism there assumed a 'normality' so permanent that it aborts final solution? It is already three years since Senator George Mitchell flew in from Washington to act as a mediator using legendary diplomatic skills. No decommissioning of weapons would lessen the meaning of terrorism in Northern Ireland. What was really needed, he believed, was a 'decommissioning of mind-sets' (*Belfast Telegraph*, 26 April 1996).

The second example of the need for wider examination is that of contemporary Spain. The persistence of terrorism among Basques in the north presents an enigma. The Basques are a proud national group whose desire for autonomy was cruelly subjugated by the dictator Franco during the 1930s. In the minds of many Basques, resort to guerrilla warfare against Madrid became morally justifiable and for the past 40 years they have rallied to ETA, the Basque Revolutionary Movement of National Liberation. As ardent liberationists were cut down mercilessly by security forces, the guerrillas turned away from military targets and became terrorists bombing and shooting bank clerks in raids. Civilian Basques were murdered. Predictably, the majority of Basques now see indiscriminate violence as counter-productive. Indeed, Basques have already been granted a measure of constitutional autonomy. For most Basques terrorism might be defined as something they do not want.

State sponsored terrorism

Traditionally, terrorism has been perceived as a two-way contest between a band of violent activists and a sovereign state. The contemporary world throws a spotlight on certain states which are keen to use terrorist organisations to promote their interests internationally. President George Bush has referred to these states as 'rogue states' orchestrating terrorism as an 'axis of evil' and he has named them as Afghanistan, Syria, Libya, Sudan and North Korea. Intelligence sources in the United States use a two-fold classification:

- States which carry out terrorist acts beyond their own borders to advance political objectives. Civilians and civilian facilities are routinely attacked.
- States which assist terrorist organisations with political and ideological support, funding and various forms of material assistance.

These patron states use their beneficiaries as puppets to spread their own ideology. This way strategic goals can be approached more cheaply and effectively than by deploying armed force.

Once more, the absence of consensual definition at the international level hampers effective counter-terrorism. There is little prospect of international collaboration to curb the sponsoring states whatever the heartfelt wishes of the Bush Administration. In many cases, sponsoring governments are authoritarian and their peoples complacent, even sympathetic, as many Muslims are, about attacks on the Great Satan of the West. In any case, the criteria by which the United States and Israel, for instance, judge the violence of Hizbullah and Hamas are not shared by many Arabs, most obviously in the Lebanon and Syria. For Palestinians it is Israel's punitive strikes against their towns and farmlands that put that country into the category of 'state terrorist'. Many sponsoring states in the Middle East see terrorist activities as a *jihad*, a sanctified mission to fight against heresy and the infidel West. Terrorism may be defined as a redeeming pan-Islamic struggle.

Could sponsoring states do more to dissuade their clients from persisting with activities which the rest of the world regards as heinous and unpardonable? There is some evidence that this is already happening. Libya, once infamous for its training camps and combat courses for 'subversives', has come out of the cold. If oil marketing replaces terrorist export, Quaddafi's Libya will be richer and safer. A United States air strike in 1986 and United Nations sanctions convinced terrorists and their backers that the market-place is to be preferred to the bunker and a likely hangman's noose.

It was noted after the New York outrage that certain states previously considered terrorist-inclined were ready, so they said, to join Washington's anti-terrorist coalition. They included Sudan, Iran, Syria, Egypt, Indonesia and Libya.

The scale of definition

A troubled world, searching for consensus about the meaning of terrorism and how to counter it, finds it impossible to frame a workable definition. Meanwhile, the word 'terrorism' is on every-body's lips, in every news-sheet and flashed across TV screens. We all use the term and nobody explains it adequately, though this is not for want of trying. What there are in the main are bald refer-ences to intentional causes and horrific consequence.

There seems to be general acknowledgement, nevertheless, that contemporary terrorists are now operating globally and on a rising scale. The New York attack yielded the biggest body-count ever. Bali, the tourist paradise, was catastrophically laid waste. The highly secretive network of al-Qaida represents a potent, demonic mission recruiting, it is thought, from 50 to 60 existing terrorist organisations in more than 50 lands. Its ideological militancy, forged by the Soviet invasion of Afghanistan in 1979 and the link with fundamentalist Taliban, has had an appeal resonating for more than a decade throughout the Islamic world. A result of this is the fielding of desperate key players determined to oust Western and chiefly United States influence from their Middle Eastern heartlands. It would be tragic if the wave of condemna-tion after 9/11 were to turn into flaring hostility between the West and the Islamic world.

Concern about the scale of terrorism is more than ever focussed on the fear that terrorists here and there may acquire chemical and biological weapons and even the small-scale 'nuclear suitcase'. The impact of this speculation will be examined later in Chapter 9. For the moment a search for meaning comes up against crude reality. The world on its doorstep and the world with its people faces mega-risk and mega-terrorism. That part of the definition at least is plain.

This chapter is by far the shortest chapter in this book. It is so because it is designed as a 'taster', as an introduction to something that may not be easy to digest. Definition is, of course, the begin-ning of things and, ideally, a brief explanation of the precise meaning of a word. If precision eludes us, for some of the reasons already stated, it may be possible to work out a reasonable mean-ing when a number of aspects of terrorism are discussed. The chapters that follow discuss geographical contexts, motivation and terrorists banded in groups or acting in isolation. Prominence is given to media image, to common ethical and moral issues, and to future forms of terrorism. Hopefully, these chapters will fill out a discussion of terrorism and terrorists which can be summarised in Chapter 11.

Already, as we try to define terrorism in the contemporary world, we have to wrestle with the paradox that if terrorism is growing more and more globalised it is what individual terrorists do and hope to achieve that puts a kernel into meaning.

2 Terrorism today and yesterday

Terrorism's dispersion and scale

This chapter will address a number of questions. Where are terrorists operating in the contemporary world? What is the scale of their operations? What, in outline, are the historical roots of what we term as terrorism? Lastly, and disturbingly, is the work of terrorists edging us towards wider confrontations, for instance, between the West and the Islamic world?

The dispersion of terrorism

The map (pp. 14–15) illustrates the general dispersion of recorded terrorist activities. What might be thought of as 'flash points' or 'hot spots' are now to be found in every continent. Something like 70 states are affected by the nefarious activities of at least 100 terrorist groups, diverse in character and membership. The contemporary world has to reckon with networking by perhaps 20,000 to 30,000 terrorists widely dispersed, according to the Institute of Strategic Studies. This chapter offers only a geographical outline of this dispersion. There is a comprehensive list of terrorist groups in Appendix II, while Appendix III is a chronology, surveying years during which terrorist activities were most marked. Detailed description of the more significant groups will be found in Chapter 3. Chapter 4 will take a close look at terrorist motivation, and tactics and methods are considered in Chapter 6.

It used to be the case that terrorists were a threat largely to states which saw their problem as an isolated one, whether it took the form of occasional incidents or that of a sustained campaign.

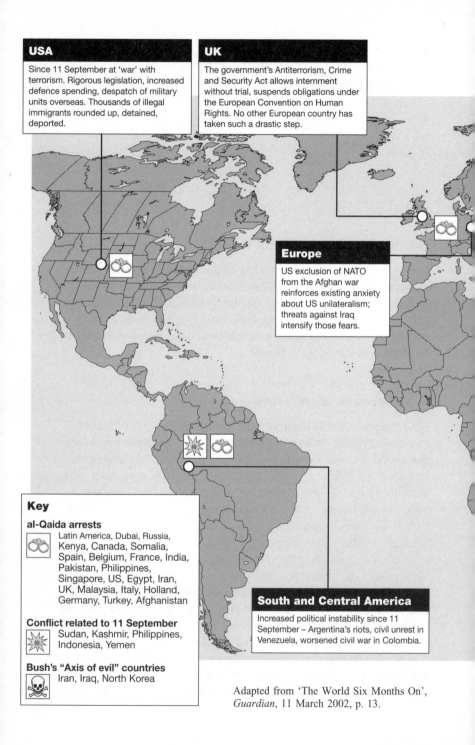

USA

Since 11 September at 'war' with terrorism. Rigorous legislation, increased defence spending, despatch of military units overseas. Thousands of illegal immigrants rounded up, detained, deported.

UK

The government's Antiterrorism, Crime and Security Act allows internment without trial, suspends obligations under the European Convention on Human Rights. No other European country has taken such a drastic step.

Europe

US exclusion of NATO from the Afghan war reinforces existing anxiety about US unilateralism; threats against Iraq intensify those fears.

Key

al-Qaida arrests

Latin America, Dubai, Russia, Kenya, Canada, Somalia, Spain, Belgium, France, India, Pakistan, Philippines, Singapore, US, Egypt, Iran, UK, Malaysia, Italy, Holland, Germany, Turkey, Afghanistan

Conflict related to 11 September

Sudan, Kashmir, Philippines, Indonesia, Yemen

Bush's "Axis of evil" countries

Iran, Iraq, North Korea

South and Central America

Increased political instability since 11 September – Argentina's riots, civil unrest in Venezuela, worsened civil war in Colombia.

Adapted from 'The World Six Months On', *Guardian*, 11 March 2002, p. 13.

Israeli/Palestinian territories

Could the events of 11 September provide the brutal shock to dislodge all sides from their cycle of violence? Now that hope fades.

Arab world

All Arab states formally condemned the 11 September attacks though most criticised the ensuing Afghanistan war.

Russia

A fundamental shift in foreign policy moves Russia closer to the US with far-reaching implications for the west.

China

US-China relations much improved now that Washington has a new enemy.

North Korea

Included in Bush's 'axis of evil' despite their condemning terrorism. Accused of preparing mass-destruction weapons. North-south peace process now set back.

Afghanistan

Since Taliban demise in November 2000 warlord rivalry, lawlessness, fragile government threaten civil war.

South-east Asia

Several governments using war on terror as excuse to crack down on internal dissenters e.g. US 'hit squads' active against Philippine rebels.

Iraq/Iran

Iraq named in 'axis of evil' and so in firing line. Iran opposed both bin Laden and Taliban but lumping with Iraq and North Korea probably strengthened position of hardliners opposing rapprochement with the west.

India/Pakistan

India moves against own 'terrorists' in Kashmir, introduces draconian anti-terrorist laws. Pakistan rewarded with US aid for endorsing US Afghan bombing. India demands end to covert support of Islamic militants.

Correspondingly, counter-terrorism was organised on *ad hoc*, piecemeal lines, tidying up afterwards and searching for those thought to be responsible. Only during the last few years has terrorism in the world today been thought about as a global threat calling for global counter-action. This point will be considered in later chapters.

Primarily, Middle Eastern countries constitute a zone of anguish and have done so for most of a century. Many of these lands were in thrall to the British and French empires and resentment at their exploitation and some religious or sectarian difference led to outbursts of infighting which could be anaesthetised by punitive expeditions. Rarely was Islamic anger directed at 'infidels' from the West and there were never any strikes directed at their home-lands. Today's Middle East, as everybody knows, is exploding in violence, with much of it being carried into the heartlands of what is understood as a hostile West. A major factor making for polit-ical violence being endemic in this region is, of course, the fortress posture of Israel under daily siege from Arab radicals. There is no sign there of any peaceful settlement. A more recent growth of political violence is that of the flood of anti-American feelings focused on the coalition assault on Saddam Hussein's Iraq. There is every chance that the military strike has already reactiv-ated the smouldering readiness to sponsor terrorists that lingers in Iran, Syria, Libya and Saudi Arabia and added to the coming apart of a rather tenuous Arab unity, when more extreme elements turn inwards and berate any Arab government siding with the United States.

South East Asia has many people resentful at economic depen-dence on capitalist states. Anger and frustration turn easily into strife. The fact that authoritarian governments come down heavily on any expression of dissent tends to make for differences of opinion flaring into violence. There are also in Indonesia and the Philippines strong Islamic affiliations which underscore the intent and devotion of many who would resort to terror acts. On occa-sion, each of these states has been accused by the United States of not doing enough to forestall terrorist acts. (American and Australian critics have alleged that what happened at Bali in October 2002 need never have happened if Jakarta had been more awake to possible dangers.) A source of great tension and disorder in the region is Afghanistan, where a fragile peace accord is troubled by sectarian feuding. Neighbouring Pakistan is teetering on the edge of lawlessness and is a sanctuary, so it is reported, for terrorist elements of al-Qaida and the Taliban who have left their earlier fastness in Afghanistan. To the west is Kashmir, at present a hotbed of intrigue and planned violence in the eyes of Delhi.

Central and South America are at present less fought over than was the case two decades ago. Economic imbalance and uncertainty lie at the heart of most instability in this region. While there are still tensions just below boiling point, the pot is simmering in Honduras, Guatemala, Argentina, Peru, Bolivia and Chile. It is in Colombia that violence continues to tear a community apart, much of it related to narcotics production and dealing. The reconciliation attempts there of the late 1990s, which promised to put an end to 50 years of internal strife, cannot be said to have taken a firm hold yet. Aspects of some of this New World terrorism will be examined in later chapters. Europe's terrorism, one might say, is either eradicated or is in suspense. In contemporary Germany and Italy there are few out in the open who would be prepared to follow the 'justificational violence' which was the mantra of groups such as Germany's Baader-Meinhof and the Red Army Faction or Italy's Brigate Rosse in the 1960s and 1970s. Terrorism there faded away as the result of a strange and wavering coincidence when government handling became more robust, public pressure grew more sustained and there was an increased sense of futility among terrorists. Small cells of determined ex-terrorists lurk here and there, to be sure, doubtless waiting for a cause célèbre. Active terrorism in today's Europe is located in Northern Ireland and in the Basque region of Northern Spain. These scenarios are enigmatic in that they represent conflicts once lacerated by violence and then nearing solution through a peace process which has taken a fragmentary hold. In these two places, as Chapter 3 will show, there is a terrorist potential, dependent in Northern Ireland on the demilitarisation of paramilitary groups in the forefront of a deeper sectarian divide and in Spain on the eventual outcome of finite negotiations following a ceasefire.

In the wider world, and a point made in Chapter 1, there is concern about so-called 'rogue states' whose pro-active interest in terrorism or the support of it at long range represents a danger. An often repeated litany of distrust embraces North Korea, Iran, Syria, Libya and the Yemen.

The scale of terrorism

© Andrzej Krauze

The scale of contemporary terror has escalated just as its dispersion has expanded. A rough estimate of its scale may be gleaned from library sources. Since 1968 there have been at least 8,000 serious incidents. It is the major incident whose drama stands starkly in the headlines and there have been at least 150 of these. However, it is the drip feed of incident on incident – the bombs, the suicide fanatics, the car bombs, kidnapping and group hostage taking, assassination, air hijacking, gas attacks – that present a terrible scourge mainly for an innocent and unprepared public. A minimum count of casualties over three decades would be of the order of 5,500 fatalities and 19,000 injured, some of whom have been crippled for life. A number of major incidents, including those in Kenya and in New York, have seen hundreds, if not several thousands, killed. Added to this toll is the tremendous cost of carnage in money, disruption to daily life and services, in clearance and rebuilding. Terrorists bring trauma to the streets, and fear and anger among victims and witnesses.

Wide dispersion and increasing scale demonstrate the increasing vulnerability of all nations. Nobody, anywhere, can any longer feel safe. Distance is no longer protecting us in a shrinking world, where the battlefield is global and the old distinction between combatant and non-combatant seems on an abstract plane. It was noticeable that the chaos of 9/11 momentarily unified world opinion. Terror stressed interdependence for, as *Le Monde* in Paris put it, 'We are all Americans now'.

Terrorism's historical roots

A number of historical vantage points can be picked out, for instance:

* terrorism in antiquity
* terrorism and the French Revolution
* terrorism and Tsarist Russia
* terrorism 1900 to 1945
* terrorism and anti-colonialism
* terrorism and protest
* terrorism and separatism.

Today's events and something of the future are only really understandable if one looks back now and then. It certainly helps to understand the characteristics and significance of contemporary terrorism if some of its historical roots are thought about.

Terrorism in antiquity

The terrorism of antiquity has given us a number of terms still used in the modern era. Zealot, assassin, thug, are such terms used mainly in condemnation. Zealots demonstrated nationalistic and religious fervour in the first century AD in the Holy Land provinces of the Roman Empire. They put Roman soldiers and officials to the dagger, the sica, and they occasionally torched the houses of fellow Jews whom they considered to be heretics or collaborators. The fanaticism of these terrorists broadcast a message of undying resistance to the Roman occupation of their ancestral lands and a threat to anyone tempted to deviate from narrow orthodox lines of Jewish belief.

Assassins were devotees of a Muslim cult, the Shi'ite Order of Assassins, sworn to expel Christian invaders of Palestine during the eleventh and twelfth century crusades. They roamed in small bands through modern Syria, Iraq and Israel, hunting Christian infidels and also murdering Sunni Muslims whose beliefs and rituals they found detestable. This dedicated mission group bears an uncanny parallel to today's Hizbullah bombers coming out of Lebanon and to the Tamil Tigers of Sri Lanka. Success and suicide for ancient and modern assassins ensure a place in Paradise as well as veneration as a martyr.

Thugs in modern parlance are usually thought of as brutal ruffians. Originally, they were a cult of fanatics, spreading terror throughout central and northern India for almost 1,200 years until the British Raj marked them down with expeditionary forces in the mid-1800s. Their cause, if one can describe it so, was partly religious and partly banditry. Their speciality was sacrificial strangulation to placate the bloodthirsty Hindu goddess Kali. Sometimes disguised as market traders, the thugs seem to have selected many thousands of victims indiscriminately. The practice of *thugee* petrified white residents in India and led to much sensational discussion back in imperial Britain. This particular viciousness has gone but it is disconcerting that a long-held readiness to associate terrorists with a mysterious east resonates today among those quick to point to lands east of Gibraltar as harbouring murder and deceit.

Terrorism and the French Revolution

Terrorism at the time of the French Revolution in the late 1790s accentuated political goals in an unusual fashion. Leaders of the Revolution were desperate to clamp down on dissent. In 1793–4 they employed not only the guillotine to get rid of opponents, but fear itself. Quite deliberately a reign of terror (*la régime de la terreur*) was instituted to consolidate a fragile government and to intimidate all who might deny it its hard-won, newly-found power. Robespierre was something of a callous, passionate terrorist himself. He calculated that a people frightened about being named, arrested and summarily disposed of would easily come to heel. Terror, as an instrument of governance, would confer virtue, justice and a sense of order upon citizens, promoting and defending the Right against the Wrong (Hoffman 1999: 16). Modern regimes which have put in place a regime of terror have always been dictatorial. Many later examples of this come to mind – Nazi Germany, Fascist Italy, the Stalinist Soviet Union, Pol Pot's Khmer Rouge, Saddam Hussein's Iraq and Pinochet's Chile.

Terrorism and Tsarist Russia

Terrorism in Tsarist Russia was in most respects the converse of that of revolutionary France. Robespierre had the notion of safeguarding through terror methods 'the will of the people'. One hundred years later, terrorism was taken up against Tsarist autocracy and corruption. A group of determined Russians, chiefly students and intellectuals, became convinced that only violent subversion would fight state denial of liberty. A well-planned campaign, in essence the People's Power (*Narodnaya Volya*), was to rock the foundations of imperial power and of inflexible bureaucracy, and would surely free Russians from their yoke. If this meant the assassination of the monarch and systematic targeting of the enemies of the people then this would be a small price to pay for the transfer of property and the liberation of the serfs. Mother Russia was to be given back to its deserving people. Governments and many in the courts of Europe lost no time in calling the Russian freedom fighters 'inhuman anarchists'. In fact, although these resolute activists resorted to the pistol and the bomb, they proclaimed humanity in not wanting to shed blood unnecessarily. It so happened that innocent bystanders did become casualties and a number of planned incidents failed. It was after the murder of Tsar Alexander II in March 1881 that Government resources in the army and the secret police broke the strength and resolve of protestors and prevented the wave of civil unrest spreading much beyond the cities of Moscow and St Petersburg. Russia had to wait many years before the Bolshevik Revolution of 1917. It was that event rocking many boats in Europe in its tremendous groundswell of public debate and apprehension that led to many in politics, who claimed allegiance as socialists, communists and their allied groups, being vilified, quite mistakenly, as 'terrorists'.

Terrorism 1900 to 1945

Political contest was the hallmark of terrorism in the first decade of the twentieth century. Its focus moved to the east and south eastern fringes of Europe. The Ottoman and Habsburg Empires were thought of as despotic and deserving elimination by nationalist agitators in Serbia, Bulgaria, Greece and Turkey. Much of this was condemned as the insufferable, irresponsible activity of anarchists, radicals and socialists, together with the observation that their links and their controllers in London, Paris and Berlin must be identified. The early years of the century were years of rising tension and frustrated popular hopes. Violence as a strategy headed many agendas both with governments planning for war and with demonstrators convinced that only robust, often destructive, action could claim public attention and hopefully some redress. Violence as a tactic, though, did not always yield profitable results. The assassination of President McKinley in 1901 shocked the American public just as it had when President Garfield was shot in 1881. Opinions held that these outrages were the work of deranged individuals and not the deliberate policy of a definite anti-state group (Laqueur 1999: 265). The trauma of terror on this occasion was temporary. More ominously, for those who thought that careful political activism might use only the minimum of force to make a point, it was a pistol shot and an Archduke's murder in Sarajevo that led to allied and central powers marching to war in August 1914.

Terrorism took a new turn in the 1920s and 1930s. Throughout Europe there was a great deal of dissatisfaction and turmoil as the hopes raised by the conclusion of the First World War turned sour. Terrorism began to acquire a new significance, becoming institutionalised where power-seeking cliques were ruthlessly out for political change. Strongarm methods, violating basic human rights, were the rule in Germany, Italy, Japan, Poland, Romania, Greece and Hungary. One set of distinctive ideological principles was to be enforced. To ensure discipline and order, the jackboots and armbands of hit squads were everywhere on the streets. The Brown Shirts, the Black Shirts and the Iron Guard of the extreme political Right fought running battles with not only the Reds of the Left but with anyone picked out as liberal or belonging to a despised ethnic minority. Where brute force ousted the ballot box, the disenfranchised had little choice than to respond with counter-terror. Those of them who survived iron fist repression were lauded as patriots and their resort to violence excused. The terror of these years increasingly became 'techno-terrorism' using radio and 24-hour printing machinery. There was no place for compromise or debate.

It was in the 1930s, a time of defeatism and economic slump, that terrorism developed dramatically and on a major scale as an instrument of state power. The fascism of Hitler, Mussolini and Franco prospered only if it mobilised the masses physically and symbolically. Unity, power and strength had to be realised through discipline and subordination. A cohort of tough followers storm-trooped through town and countryside. Their terror use was the justifiable equipment of he-who-must-be-obeyed. Worse still, in 1937 the Nazis rained terror from the skies over Spain and, similarly, Mussolini over Ethiopia. Hitler marched terror into Austria in 1938 and across the Czechoslovak frontier in 1938 and again in 1939. Terror was the export commodity of a growth industry.

The ensuing world war between 1939 and 1945 knew no bounds of human observance. Total war bred total terror. Terror was a vital ingredient of much that took place – the Nazi occupation of the bulk of Europe, the deliberate, covert hit and run of the Resistance, and the barbarism of genocide. Terrorism in many forms engulfed the peoples of Europe and Asia, now bringing civilians in places on to the battlefield. There was indiscriminate bombing and fire-storming of enemy air forces, culminating in what has been described as the ultimate terrorist incident, the nuclear incineration of Hiroshima and Nagasaki. Tackling a ruthless enemy who ignored Geneva Conventions often led to in-humane methods of attack and defence which were explained away as unavoidable. Inevitably, at the Nuremberg Trials in 1945, defeated German generals and political leaders were arraigned, many of them, as terrorists-in-uniform. It was also said at the time that had the other side won then there was a real prospect that certain Allied leaders, reluctant terrorists, maybe, would have been seated in the dock.

Terrorism and anti-colonialism

With peace at last in 1945, terrorism, as violent political activism, took on new meanings. Violence was to be a shot in the locker for those setting out to demolish at all costs the imperial rule of Britain, France, the Netherlands and Portugal, in Africa and Asia. These were freedom fighters in the admiring view of masses hun-gry for emancipation. London, Paris, The Hague and Lisbon saw them as terrorists breaking the colonial rule of law, terrorists to be hunted and imprisoned. No effort was to be spared to protect colonial outposts from attack by the 'wicked' and the 'uncivilised'. Eventually the determination of the movers and shakers won the day and self-determination was accorded to colonial dependencies the world over (though never too willingly).

Out of the fire of the liberators, political violence was in some measure given a new face. Descent to the use of terrorist methods was deplored but the general thrust for a people's freedom in Palestinian territories or apartheid South Africa was approved this time by numerous members of the United Nations. It had to be conceded in the Old World that the new Third (Developing) World would never have been born if their struggles had been 100 per cent non-violent. Liberationist zeal transgressed moral boundaries but such excesses were pardonable. Independence had been won. How could anyone fighting to free kinsfolk from oppression ever be called a terrorist, with all its negative associations, was a question voiced by Nelson Mandela (Mandela 1997: 626).

Terrorism and protest

All terrorists are protestors. History shows that protest which is unheeded by authority can lead to outbreaks of violence which are then commonly interpreted as being terrorist. During the last 40 or so years of the twentieth century, three major instances of collective protest turning sour and vicious were those in Germany, Italy and Argentina. In many respects these three scenarios were quite different but we can learn a lot from them.

Germany in the late 1960s was making commendable progress drawing away from its Nazi past. There were vibrant feelings of enterprise and democracy on every hand. It was among students that protest became loud. Their universities were stifled by bureaucracy. Civic reform lacked vision and pace. The official socialist parties and certainly their leaders were old-fashioned and undependable. Against the urgings of such inspirational figures as Henri Marcuse and Jean-Paul Sartre the future of a brave new Germany seemed already unpromising. Out in the wider world there was the American violation of Vietnam, the manipulations of NATO, the scourge of nuclear weaponry and the exploitation of the capitalist system. Protest needed to be taken to barricades and the possibility of armed struggle. That would get them publicity as a prelude to forcing change, if not speedy improvements.

At the centre of the gathering storm was a group of fierce campaigners calling themselves the Red Army Faction (some of them belonging to a Baader-Meinhof clique). They would constitute an extra-parliamentary opposition. Two hundred active members flocked in from professional and academic families, not so many from workers. By 1970 one in three of them were young women. Confrontation with the police brought casualties and anger. Stones and Molotov cocktails were replaced with bombs, sniping with rifles, and large-scale arson, in Frankfurt, Berlin and Hamburg. Protest had flamed into deliberate reliance on terror methods and the picking out of victims – a leading industrialist, a judge, a newspaper editor, a banker and any NATO personnel. A second wave of young terrorists took over in the 1980s. In 1986 alone there were 400 serious terror incidents. Hunger strikes were a successful way of ensuring newspaper headlines.

It was into the 1990s that German terrorism began to cool off. Partly, this seems to have been a consequence of a failure to recruit intelligent youth rather than loutish ones. Red Army Faction goals, as they were put about, began to appear less rational and with an element of fantasy. Clearly, that was how most Germans were beginning to see it as the end of the 1980s approached. To begin with, there had been fear and panic. This gave way to an increasing view of the terrorists as senseless, trigger-happy zealots who were easily rounded up by the police and whose message rang ever more incoherently. How could a dedicated few ever suppose that comradeship with the world's downtrodden would have any magnetic appeal if it took the form of end-justifies-the-means violence? When terrorist propaganda shifted from justifying a genuine popular struggle to calling for deliberate attacks on people and property, was this not then going to be thought destructive and nihilistic? The interesting thing about this German experience is that not only did the security forces contain the protest with great efficiency (and never too light-handedly) but they were backed up by a citizenry that was anxious to dispel any association of their young post-war democracy with terror methods. Terrorism was to be outlawed.

The Italian experience between 1970 and 1990 presents a contrast. There was a middle-class, student component, as in Germany, but radical Italians wanted to take on a government which struck them as a bourgeois dictatorship. Government 'violence', that is, repressive violation of human rights, would have to be met with justified violence, regardless of cost. The calling themselves the Red Brigade, Brigate Rosse, the protestors came in from traditional activist outlets in Italy, namely, communist and reformist Catholics, together with a number of seasoned wartime resistance fighters. Ardour and energy were fuelled by long spells of unemployment and social malaise. Their strategy was to be a cat and mouse wearing down of politicians they saw as ineffectual, divided and corrupt. The campaign would be clandestine and without scruples. The bomb and the rifle would shatter official complacency. Arms could be obtained from Angola, Libya, Cuba or Czechoslovakia where there were training camps for men of violence.

The terrorists seem to have miscalculated their mission and its likely success in several ways. It might have been that Italians in general appeared so cynical about their Rome government that they could be expected to learn to live with isolated outrages against state power. They might fatalistically shrug their shoulders when it was seen that, after all, terror methods were in the armoury of both the political left and the political right. Weak counter-terrorism tactics by the government would strengthen the popular image of feasible reform-through-violence. These proved mistaken ideas. The kidnapping of Aldo Moro, a former Prime Minister, and his murder, back in 1978, horrified all sections of society. Moro's captors were surely criminals. No excess of political enthusiasm could excuse that and the 14,000 Brigate Rosse attacks between 1970 and 1987. It was not long before popular perceptions unified to brand the Brigate Rosse as locked into a vicious cycle of violence where there was no rational message. Terror strategies were mindless, destructive and non-negotiable. Italy and Germany had finished with terrorism on a major scale by the end of the last century. Even so, there remain today small factions ready to terrorise if they need to – a neo-Nazi gathering in Germany, and in Italy some neo-Fascist elements allied with the Mafia.

Argentina's experience of terrorism has been described as 'enigmatic and macabre' (Whittaker 2003: 120). The lives of 34 million people alternated over 30 years between the early 1950s and the late 1980s from hope to despair. There were the exciting promises of the charismatic Juan Perón for a brighter, more egalitarian dynamic to begin with, only to be dashed after a coup in 1955 with a succession of military juntas, fierce and corrupt, that elbowed each other out of the way. Bitterness and frustration led to enmity fracturing the country and sparking violence. Argentina became a free-for-all battleground of feuding with individuals and groups seeking vengeance, political factions settling old scores, and state-sponsored 'heavy squads' terrorising the streets to root out 'subversions'.

A small knot of students came together around 1968 determined to recreate an Argentina that offered freedom of opportunity, equality and social justice. Many of them were staunchly Catholic, most of them claiming to be fiercely nationalistic, and few of them were socialists. They took the name Montoneros, which traditionally referred to a romantic picture of range-riding horsemen. Revering the memory of Perón, they were the political-cum-military vanguard of a popular revolution. For 'Power to the People' to succeed, intellectual and ideological muscle was needed rather than firearms, for combat would be essentially 'defensive'. This declaration of the Montoneros' early days attracted several thousand to a 'revolutionary advance'.

As always, so it seems, the heady first days develop into stalemate, internal dispute, disenchantment and the risky attempts to meet firepower with firepower. Initially, the Montoneros espoused the 'urban guerrilla' tactics of Che Guevara to liberate and incorporate those in town or on the ranches who would surely flock to the colours. Civilian casualties would be minimal. Weakness as a result of being on the run, and deprivation, began both to erode the Montoneros' ranks and confidence. Argentinians, on the whole, were less apathetic and fatalistic than the Italians. No doubt, their expectations had been aroused by propaganda so that when reform fell short of target, disappointment took the shape of 'look the other way – don't get involved' and even some sympathy for counter-terror measures despite State security action being normally draconian. Lack of progress for the protestors inevitably led to their use of terror methods and ultimately to their demise.

Argentina has not yet recovered from its brutal past. The era of terror was succeeded in 1982 by the disastrous conflict with Britain over the Falkland Islands. At least, the aftermath of that was to oust the dictator General Galtieri and to usher in a more stable democracy. The tally of terrorism was enormous with over 2,000 killed,

10,000 imprisoned, perhaps 30,000 'disappearances'. Argentinians remain sickened and saddened by political terrorism bringing a whole nation to insecurity and suffering.

Terrorism and separatism

The Cold War imprisoned East–West allegiances within a perma-freeze until in 1980 the Berlin Wall was hacked down in a peaceful gesture. Most terrorist groups had been revolutionary 'hard left' groups chipping away at the edges of a political glacier. With the unfreezing of 35 years of political stalemate the claims of ethno-nationalist, separatist groups were voiced with increasing stridency in all parts of Africa, in Indonesia, Cyprus and then in the Balkans and among the new republics of Russia's eastern fringe. Certainly, new states joining the United Nations as members had less reason than ever to use terror as an enabling device to secure autonomy. What happened was that separatist groups within states from Quebec to Manila in the Philippines urged their own claims to self-determination. Terrorist incidents, though, hardly earned them credibility. The violent tactics of some paramilitaries in Northern Ireland, the arson of the Basque ETA, bombing in Kashmir and Sri Lanka, the infighting in Kosovo, seemed an impetuous descent down the slope of reason.

No government in Tel Aviv, Madrid or Moscow was prepared to make political concessions to those who substituted high explosive and the suicide kit for diplomacy. On the other hand these governments could scarcely ignore that in the world outside there was often sympathy, either mute or loud-voiced, for what seems a struggle for freedom. For years the United States sought to contain with drastic force what it understood was rampant Marxism in Vietnam, Cambodia, Nicaragua and San Salvador and at the same time had to endure loud liberal disapproval from elsewhere.

A historical sketch of terrorism as a disquieting phenomenon shows its mixed ancestry, at times dishonourable, at other times evidence of a fight for liberty and human rights. An alarming thought is that many contemporary terrorists go far beyond the limits of humane and discriminating behaviour. This behaviour is beyond any law. Success for the terrorist is often through death and destruction. Demonstrating this earns maximum publicity.

There is nothing new in this since the days of antiquity. What is new, however, is the dispersion of terrorism and the scale of its operation.

Terrorism as world confrontation

The last question this chapter raises is one much talked about in 2003. Are we on the verge of terrorists pitting, say, the West against Islam? Is there a conspiracy? Are global confrontations somewhere in the manuals of the politically violent? It was after 9/11 that an expected furore of speculation arose. The New York hijackers were from the Middle East. So were those who had outraged America by damaging their interests in Kenya and Tanzania, Aden and Indonesia. More than any gut reaction, the announced message from Washington was 'this means war', above all against the man who had declared war on America, Osama bin Laden, and his al-Qaida terrorists. And they were Middle Easterners. Apart from a welter of debate in the press, academic discussion is fierce but not always too cogent or helpful. In the United States, Harvard Professor Samuel Huntington upset liberals in 1996 with his apparently deterministic notion of a 'clash of civilisations' (Huntington 1996: *passim*). More recently, he believes that any clash would consist of a series of 'rearguard actions' from a society whose traditional existence was threatened by modernisation, and implies that such a clash need not be mutually destructive to East and West (Huntington 2002: 9–13). Edward Said, an eminent Muslim authority, has attempted some bridge building in answer to Huntington by declaring that confrontations, the result of terrorism, are a dialogue of the death, a shouting match with closed eyes and suspended thought. He implies that, because terrorism is the tool of the weak and never of the strong, we have to go out and meet with our minds and actions those who are over there behind the terrorists. This is a challenge but not a life-threat. The roots of violence in major cultures must be examined (Said 1998: *passim*).

A hopeful sign is that there is a readiness, in many quarters, to understand what it is like for 300 million people in the Middle East to live daily with ethnic hostilities, loss of land, unassured access to fresh water, despotic misrule and denial of human rights.

Each country in the region has its web of frustration. To take one example of deprivation, Saudi Arabia's autocratic regime lords over 23 million Arabs, half of whom are under 25 years old and half of whom are jobless. Saudi Arabia exports oil and terrorists and that surprises nobody.

The year 2003 opened with two ominous worries for the world. First, the threat of Islamic alienation both in the Middle East and among Muslims resident in the West, should further military intervention follow on from that of the United States in Afghanistan the previous year. A likely attack on Iraq, though not directly linked with terrorism, was seen as pouring petrol on combustible materials. (This seems an apt analogy, bearing in mind that 10 of the 11 OPEC oil producers are Muslim states.)

The other anxiety at the beginning of 2003 was the arresting of terrorist suspects in Britain, Italy, France, Spain and Germany. Police units took away weapons, bomb making packs, forged passports and credit cards and some canisters of chemicals. In Britain house searches came across traces of ricin, a deadly poison. Liaison between European intelligence services was reported to be tightening on a suspected network of those planning to launch terror campaigns in 'sensitive target areas'. This was a sign once more that terrorists were dispersing their operations. Links with the al-Qaida organisation (now thought to exist in at least 50 countries) were thought to be at the root of the dispersion. Most of the arrested were from North Africa, chiefly from Algeria and Morocco.

In summary, the geographical spread of terrorism illustrates contrast and negates any notion of universality. From Greece and Egypt to the Philippines and Japan, from Iran, Iraq and Libya to Northern Ireland, Spain and Cambodia, there have been multi-coloured phases of violent political activity, different in origin, organisation, and sometimes changed emphasis and method.

Already, the conclusion seems inevitable. Generalities in our thinking must give way to territorial focusing. In the face of the wide dispersion and increasing scale of terrorism, the prospect of global war as a panacea will have to give way to an order of plans and priorities where individual states are helped to locate and eventually eradicate terrorist acts. Greece has already planned to deploy 50,000 security personnel to guard the Athens Olympics in 2004 at a cost of £510 million. With hijacking and assassination attempts, on-the-spot force may well be the only way of coping.

Otherwise, with the legal backing of conventions, the International Court and tribunal agreements (and these exist universally), what is essentially a criminal act is dealt with in the light of rationality and justice. States acting in concert can tackle the widening dispersion and scale of terrorism by sharing intelligence and surveillance. The way forward is long, tough and complex. It is feasible and it is not the way of war.

3 Terrorists in groups

The last chapter quoted an estimate that terrorists were operating in at least 70 countries and that there might be as many as 100 different terrorist groups. A large number of these groups are listed in Appendix II. To illustrate something of the characteristics and mode of operation of terrorist groups it will be necessary to make a selection from the list in that Appendix and to describe these groups only in outline. Five important groups, all different in many ways, have been chosen. They are prominent in contemporary headlines and discussion:

- al-Qaida – an international terrorist network;
- Hizbullah – in Israel, known for its suicide bombers;
- Tamil Tigers – Sri Lanka, suspended now during a truce;
- ETA – Spain, partly in suspense, partly active during truce;
- IRA – Northern Ireland, largely dormant during ceasefire.

In the chapters that follow there will be further references to the motives and methods characteristic of these five groups and others.

Al-Qaida

Known widely as Terrorism Incorporated, this group tops any poll of infamy. Most people since 2001 acknowledge that it is part of an 'unholy alliance' made up of al-Qaida, its founder Osama bin Laden and the fundamentalist Taliban. Their coming together in 2001 (at least in public view) graphically heightened terrorist profile, led to the perception of global conspiracy, and, correspondingly, to a call for a universal coalition to extinguish it.

© Andrzej Krauze

The group's origin can be traced back to 1979 when the Soviet Union sent 20,000 troops to Afghanistan to rescue a pseudo-Marxist government in danger from civil unrest. Communist infidels had to be met and thrown out in the view of a number of orthodox Muslims in Egypt, the Muslim Brotherhood, who set about recruiting a task force of young Muslims. This was to be a carefully administered Office of Services. A young Saudi civil engineer, Osama bin Laden, rich and religious, was keen to fund the enterprise from his reputed fortune of $300 million, especially since the task force, joining Afghanistan's partisans, the Mujahadeen (Mujahidin), had routed the Red Army after years of dogged combat. Known as al-Qaida, 'the Base', after 1988, the battle-tried Muslim veterans could be given a fresh, wider agenda (Bodansky 2001: *passim*):

- There are a number of targets for al-Qaida to engage.
- Stand and fight for the Truth of Islam, crusading against those who defile it.
- As well-armed, highly trained adventurous mercenaries, deploy into the trouble spots of Bosnia, Kosovo, Chechnya, Algeria, not as terrorists but as liberators.
- Cleanse the sacred Arab lands of heathen invaders, such as the 20,000 American GIs quartered in bin Laden's native Saudi Arabia since the Gulf War of 1991–2. Dislodging United States firepower and barracks necessitates a ruthless mission.
- A Muslim ' duty', also a crusade, a *jihad*, is to take the battle for rightful Islam into the very tents of the Americans, whether in Europe or across the Atlantic.

- A *fatwa*, a proclamation, calls for the killing of the arch-enemy.

The New York hijacking of September 2001 pointed United States intelligence in al-Qaida's direction. The threat was international for, after all, the victims had come from 80 countries. The United States struck first at the Taliban in Afghanistan, not because this group of religious fanatics was a terrorist one but because they had given al-Qaida sanctuary. A short war in Afghanistan toppled the Taliban, though predictably it scattered the devoted ranks of al-Qaida.

What is the shape of al-Qaida? Are there thousands of terrorists-in-being out there waiting in 'sleeper cells'? What is the organisational set-up? Is it an hierarchical pyramid with bin Laden at its peak (his own head priced at a $45 million reward)? As far as can be ascertained, this highly secretive network is more of a somewhat rambling 'spaghetti' type of enterprise with a central set of committees, transnational in its spread and multinational in its membership. The centre is estimated to function over lines of control and command that connect to satellite cells in at least 50 countries throughout the Middle East, South East Asia, much of Europe (including Britain), Canada and the United States. It is supposed that there is an elaborate array of training centres, activist squads and databases. Almost certainly, funds are very considerable, some of them derived from lucrative drug-dealing in Afghanistan and elsewhere from protection rackets and devious fraud schemes.

Al-Qaida terrorists tap into emotive springs of fundamental religious belief. What they believe and what they do are Right. There are no limits, it seems, to what they feel they must undertake, nor limits to the methods they employ. Terror has its own justification. They are the terrorists, par excellence. Beating them will be impossible. Even death for them is a victory.

Much of the group identity is, naturally, as conjectural as it is fearsome. Inevitably, public perceptions linger around what is known of the persona of the demon-originator, Osama bin Laden. Public enemy no. 1 is thought to be the mastermind behind tactics that shattered hotels and embassy buildings in Kenya and Tanzania where more than 200 died. This highly-educated, Westernised and volatile radical is able to think American and is competent enough

to design (if that is the word) an outrage that is carefully calculated to achieve maximum effect. His infamous octopus-like
network can and will strike anywhere, at any time. This is the
thinking of most Western intelligence services.

Surveillance apart, what can the counter-terrorism world do
about al-Qaida? There is intense and highly secretive preventive
action in many countries. Prediction is almost impossible. Military
action, on a large scale by a mega-power, seems an inappropriate
response to 'take out' localised attacks, resulting probably in
provocation and incitement to further terror. A contest with Islam
has to be avoided. Above all, Osama bin Laden, if he is still alive,
must not be awarded a martyr's crown.

Hizbullah, The Party of God

This is another terrorist group not often out of the headlines or off
the small screen. Frequent suicide bombings and assassination,
nominally on behalf of Palestinians in Israel, fill most minds with
revulsion. Nevertheless, this is a political movement which became
a fierce terrorist group with characteristics different from others
and one that deserves scrutiny to understand its vitality and Arab
appeal:

*   Hizbullah originated in Lebanon in 1982 as a militant fringe
    of Shi'ites (Shi'ira) protesting against political and social
    deprivation.
*   It is an alliance between Muslim clerics (mullahs), unelected
    politicians, journalists and students.
*   It will combat the intolerance of the ruling clique of Western-
    ised traders and Christian parliamentarians.
*   1970s and 1980s – a civil war between a weak, largely secular
    government and dissatisfied Islamic believers consolidated the
    movement.
*   Ostensibly, the protest goals are to rid Lebanon of foreign
    influences, notably those of Israel, replacing it with a truly
    independent and religiously orthodox state.
*   The movement gains momentum as leaders focus on a need
    to assert identity among Lebanese, convinced that their govern-
    ment misunderstands and marginalises them deliberately.

- Propaganda and peaceful demonstrations are prominent, until resistance from the security forces leads to protest becoming violent.
- Internal violence continues to target another scapegoat than the Lebanese oppressor, namely the foreigner.
- Westerners are snatched as hostages from time to time. American, French and British banks and factories burned and bombed.

Sympathy is expressed by Syria and Iran who assist with high explosive, subversion experts and liberal amounts of currency.

Hizbullah had earned its wings as a purposeful terrorist group. Its origin was as a defensive and liberation force – a reactive element. Now its members were to be proactive, highly assertive, with a sense of mission. If the rest of the world, particularly in Israel, condemned them as terrorists, then the rest of the world was preferring to see them as mindless rather than as mindful and dedicated to political and social revolution.

Certainly, Hizbullah demonstrates religious fervour even if this is termed elsewhere as 'fanaticism'. It has been said the Hizbullah derives vigour and inspiration from two power-houses, the mosque and the journalist's editorial room. These are the rallying centres, the despatch bases for missionaries of 'the faithful'. It is worth bearing in mind that Islamic practice and interpretation differ somewhat from country to country in the Middle East. Lebanon's distinctive observance is that religion is politics and politics is highly religious. There is a basic dual vision from the steps of the power-houses referred to above, one that Osama bin Laden spoke of, namely, that the contemporary world falls into two camps, that of the believers (God's people) and that of the unbelievers (the Devil's people). For the devotees of al-Qaida and of Hizbullah there can be no bridge between the two. The fortification of one camp, that of orthodox Islam, defending and purifying in the name of the Koran, looks rather like a crusade in reverse. For the Hizbullah, action, if it is unsuccessful in achieving objectives, legitimates terrorist action as a way of life or death. Ultimately, violent action will bring triumph. Pragmatically, suicide keeps Israel's soldiers on long periods of expensive alert. Israeli settlements are harassed in the cause of championing the dispossessed Palestinians. Autocratic administration in Israel's towns is blown apart. Unfortunately, civilians, Jew and Arab, are blasted too. Sacrifice among the Hizbullah terrorists is no loss, rather, it represents victorious progress of the individual into heaven and honour as a martyr.

Hizbullah is known for its interest in hostage-taking although this is now less pronounced. Media dividends are rich. An anxious Western world holds its breath and wrestles with dilemmas. Are the hostages left to be butchered or held to ransom? (For Hizbullah there is more profit with the last course.) A Western government, responsible for the protection of its nationals, cannot dodge the issue. Do they refuse to yield or compromise or do they give into blackmail? Publicly, governments generally state that there will be no concessions. Media presentations heighten public unease and expectations. Privately, most foreign ministers authorise exploratory negotiations and secretive deals. Facing down rock-hard terrorists is usually something individual governments attempt without talking too much about how they will do it. From time to time, Iran or Syria will be approached to mediate in the situation. A concerted Western response has never been easy given the diversity of national interests.

Is there any prospect that Hizbullah's ardour and energy may wane? How long will the group be able to sustain its three imperatives – defending Shi'ites, promoting pan-Arabism and acting as conduit for Palestinian protection? The tireless campaigning of a well-organised group has a purpose and vitality that has resonance in neighbouring lands. In other places, observers are detecting some internal dissension. There are apparent and understandable differences of opinion between mullahs, editors and students. The front line of the group is fired up by its own enthusiasm but the terrorism has an uneven edge. In the rear of the movement are religious and lay figures urging more restraint. Terror methods earn prime publicity but will they be understandable to media watchers in the West? Even the former Hizbullah patron, Syria, is less sternly supportive, no doubt aware that the United States is now serious in its determination to hunt down terrorists and their backers. One advocate of winding down some of the momentum is Sheikh Muhammed Fadlallah, senior mullah and eminent philosopher. Hizbullah must remain resolved and united in representing Arab interests. He doubts whether these interests will be understandable to non-Arabs if the shape they take is one of impetuous violence and constant risk-taking. Why not try persuasion and a softer mode of approach to those who might then appreciate the plight of the exploited in Middle Eastern countries? There is a strong thread in Fadlallah's counsel. Violence may often be the only way of securing a goal. What might be termed 'holy terror' is a legitimate way of facing outwards while facing inwards has to take account of Arab rights to life and land.

For the present, the terrorists of Hizbullah represent violence incarnate and irreconcilable. What is beyond doubt is that their removal depends upon a lasting settlement of the bitter Palestinian–Israeli issues. It is almost beyond dispute that the United States military involvement with Iraq, in the spring of 2003, has destabilised the Middle East to a large extent and given fresh impetus to the likes of Hizbullah.

Tamil Tigers in Sri Lanka

The Liberation Tigers of Tamil Elam (LTTE) have brought 21 years of despair, destruction and misery to Sri Lanka. In several respects they are quite different from the other groups described:

- They are a separatist, liberationist group unlike the international al-Qaida and the Hizbullah fighting for the Palestinians.
- They rely on techno-terrorism using the Internet (www.tamil nation.org) to pump out propaganda and to recruit their ranks, radiating programmes from their own radio and TV studios, marketing widely videos and CDs.
- They claim adherence and financial support from a world-wide network of backers, reputedly 70 million in perhaps 40 countries.

These terrorists are a puzzle. Why do they go on with terror when there are attempts to secure a compromise and ceasefire and when some autonomy must be awarded even fanatical separatists? What is it that drives a group towards armageddon when their watchword is 'destroy everything that destroys you'?

The Tigers see history as making their case a well-founded one. Sri Lanka, formerly a British possession known as Ceylon, and Eelam to Tamils, achieved independence in 1948. The Tamils, living mainly in the north and east of the island of Sri Lanka, were a minority, one in five of a total population of 17 million. An ancient people, linked ethnically with Tamil Nadu, a province in south-east India, they were largely Hindu and rural workers. In their view, independence had asserted the domination of the Sinhalist majority, chiefly Buddhist, in the capital Colombo and the chief towns. Strong feelings of oppression on the part of the Tamils led to turbulence and riots. They were not, in fact, the only protestors against an intolerant government. There was also a Sinhalist faction, the Sinhalese People's Liberation Front, which struggled against both the government and the Tamils. Inevitably, a Tamil fighting leader emerged, one Velupillai Prabhakaran, whose early Marxist orientation became increasingly nationalistic and uncompromising. He it was, in 1976, who enlisted willing volunteers into a separatist striking force, the Tamil Liberation Tigers. To begin with, they used guerrilla tactics, concentrating on military not civilian targets. As always, though, inferiority at arms brings on frustrated wider violence. It was at this point that conventional lines of warfare merged into limitless destruction as casualties on government and terrorist sides began to mount. The neighbouring state of India, in 1987, decided that something should be done to insulate its south-eastern provinces, Tamil Nadu and Karnataka, from Tamil insurgency. The first approach would be by means of exploratory talks and a peacekeeping force sent across to Sri Lanka. If this were to fail, and eventually it did, then the Indian Army would field an expeditionary force. This intervention failed either to pacify the island or to induce Tamil Tigers to show any interest in laying down arms. Savage fighting ensued. Although the Indians gained the upper hand, occupying the Tigers' principal heartland of the Jaffna peninsula, there seemed no point at all in continuing an endless siege, and India withdrew after two years of disheartening involvement. There followed a return to a bloody civil war with the Tamil Tigers wreaking havoc on military and civilian personnel. The terrorists were increasingly seen as devilish and reckless, by the Sinhalese in Colombo. What was the point of showing any understanding of those who assassinated an Indian Prime Minister, Rajiv Gandhi, in 1991, and the Sri Lankan President Prendesa in 1993?

The Tamil Tigers, tenacious and barbarous, certainly, claim

fervently that they have a rightful cause to defend. They have always been harassed and alienated, they say, by the Sinhalese. Imperial Britain disregarded them. Independence did nothing for them. Indeed, the harshness of government repression strikes them as 'genocide', violating the most basic human rights and their response has to be via armed resistance.

It is the global growth of the Tigers that makes their case distinctive. They see themselves as a transnational entity. They believe in 'growing togetherness'. Their world presence is the LTTE International claiming a supporters' club of 70 million and backing, with vast funds and weapons procurement, the suffering and purpose of the Tamil struggle. *The Times* in 1997 spoke of the LTTE International as able to keep going indefinitely 'funded by the biggest international financial empire ever built by a terrorist organisation' (23 October 1997). One estimate of the Tigers' global income (much of it from North America and Europe) is of the order of £1.25 million a month, with about a fifth of that coming from the 50,000 Tamils resident in Britain. Nevertheless, it must be emphasised that many of the 150,000 Tamils living outside Sri Lanka have never supported terrorist activities.

There is one thing that Tamils and Hizbullah and even the IRA in Northern Ireland have in common, namely, the significance of myth and tradition. A myth that proclaims that only revolutionary struggle can reassert group identity, restore inalienable rights and promote self-determination is worth fighting for regardless of cost. A myth such as this reinforces the credibility of a group. It inspires recruits. It consolidates the zeal of those who aspire, those who campaign and those who survive. The myth of invincibility gives purpose to a struggle through terror. The myth of victory-through-destruction has persuaded 17,000 Tamil Tigers in the last 20 years to resort to suicide and to seek martyrdom. 'We are', say the suicide cult, 'married to our cyanide'. In some rather strange, deep way, Tamil myths and hopes sustain 6,000 Tigers in a remorseless wave of terror despite savage losses. Terror, too, is unisex. Half of the 'Black Panthers' are women, the 'freedom birds', who are supposed to simulate pregnancy carrying high explosive charges under bulging skirts. Terror is sophisticated using speedboats and frogmen in harbours, and the latest missiles and mortars from sources in Libya, the Ukraine and Thailand.

The tally of terrorism in Sri Lanka is horrific. No town dweller, villager, policeman or priest is safe from being gunned down or bombed. Sixty thousand Sinhalese have been slain, including a score of prominent civil servants. Tamils have suffered grievously, 10,000 of them have been killed and they have lost 32 of their front rank leaders. Counter-terrorist measures by the government have been undeniably brutal.

Rampant terrorism in Sri Lanka is slowly decimating the island. After 35 years of bitter warfare, there are now signs of stalemate. In a contest for power, both sides are beginning to see the dream of complete separatist fulfilment as shattered by the march of events. Is there not room for a federal solution giving, say, autonomy to Tamil regions as a step towards autonomy and representation in Colombo's parliament? A prelude to negotiation would be a ceasefire followed by a lifting of the ban on the LTTE, and some arrangement for Tamils to meet a government deputation for exploratory peace negotiations.

A dramatic turn of events came about in April 2002. The LTTE leader, Prabhakaran, broadcast a notice saying that he would hold a press conference in rebel-held jungle on 10 April. The government cleared the main road for the access of eager journalists. Guides would escort the visitors to a secret location. No satellite phones were allowed. An excited huddle of correspondents saw the leader, not in fatigues, but a smart shirt, emerge from his bunker to face microphones and cameras. He spoke directly. 'We are seriously considering renouncing armed struggle if a solution acceptable to the Tamil people can be worked out'. He went on to state that the LTTE had been misrepresented. 'We fight', he declared, 'for the liberation of our people. You must distinguish between what constitutes terrorism and what is a liberation struggle' (*Guardian*, 10 April 2002).

The Tigers are walking away from terrorism. There have been five sets of 'talks about talks', three in Thailand, beginning in May 2002, and later ones in Oslo and Berlin. The LTTE ban has been lifted. The ceasefire, tentative to begin with, has now taken firm hold since December 2002. Tiger envoys have gone to India thinking of using Delhi as a possible mediator if talks finally break down. In 2003 there is a mood of cautious optimism in Colombo after two decades of mayhem and despair.

ETA in Basque Spain

This is one more example of a separatist group which is still as violent as ever after several decades of terrorism. Feelings of provincial nationalism remain broken into destructive conflict. Yet, as with the Tamil LTTE, there have been ceasefires and periods of conciliation. Neither of these groups seems able to rein in extremists on the movement's flanks to achieve a lasting solution to fratricide.

The ETA group takes its name from a campaign started in 1959 in the seven Basque provinces along the northern Spanish coast. Here 7 million people live with an age-old culture and a distinctive language. ETA is an acronym for Euzkadi ta Askatasuma (Basque Homeland and Freedom), clearly a phrase that sums up the liberationist zeal of those who feel oppressed. Basque students in the mid-1970s issued a forthright five-fold demand that dictatorial Madrid make sweeping concessions towards Basque autonomy. Their demands took this shape:

- full self-determination to be an indisputable right;
- the territorial integrity of the Basque homeland was undeniable and would be stoutly defended;
- the Basque language and culture were to be revitalised, given proper acknowledgement by Spain;
- there must be an amnesty for all Basque political prisoners;
- there had to be a total withdrawal of Spanish police and army from the seven provinces.

The five demands fell on deaf ears in the Fascist realm of General Franco. More than that, Madrid's propaganda began a furious tirade of insult and recrimination against Basque 'traitors'. The ETA liberators increasingly realised that only strongarm tactics would prevail. They became terrorists, moving indiscriminately against police stations, army barracks, banks and shopping malls, all symbols of intolerant Spain. With the death of Franco in 1975, the situation for the Basques began to improve with a more generous grant of civil liberties and acknowledgement of their nationalist sentiments. In spite of this, ETA violence escalated throughout their homeland. It was as though the Basques were caught up in a destructive spiral. Nobody was to be spared.

Earlier, this book has stressed the importance of considering the context within which terrorism has its origin. Tracing causal factors can lead to simplistic conclusions; the truth is usually complex. A common view of the turbulence the Basques have suffered is to see it brought on by the transformation of society and economy in the mid-nineteenth century when the old cultural roots of farm, family and church were steadily taken over by forges and shipyards. Villages and towns were now split between a newly affluent bourgeoisie and a working class that had left small-scale husbandry. The two worked and lived apart. Social tensions became political tensions concerned very much with outwitting Madrid, a cold, calculating and distant exploiter. By the 1950s radical youth groups were joined by veterans of the Spanish Civil War of 1936–9.

A call for Basque reassertion meant a call to arms. Almost certainly the rallying cry was a mix of Marxist–Leninist principles, an aping of the anti-colonial strategies now evident in the Third World, and some fairly straight sentiments about Basque revitalisation. The traitors to Madrid would never become traitors to a proud Basque identity. There was hesitancy over the methods to be employed, eventually the tougher elements had their way and a liberation undertaking turned into a life-and-death struggle. On this point commentators differ. A fair measure of autonomy and personal freedom was now assured for the Basques. Most of them were finding prosperity and job security. How was it, then, that ETA enthusiasts became terrorists-in-the-making? Why were they now so blindly up against a wall when for the most part the majority had been clear-headed about principles and purpose?

Terrorists from ETA have been particularly active in Spain since the 1970s. It has been a rather slow descent into indiscriminate violence. Egged on by funds and weapons from Cuba, Libya, Russia and Czechoslovakia and even the IRA, ETA partisans have preferred explosive force to a rational plan for change. Big city streets in various parts of Spain have been wrecked by car bombs. Prominent political and industrial leaders have been shot. Desperados, in the public view, have taken to crime, robbing banks and carrying on extortion and 'protection' rackets. Anyone too obviously Spanish or French is soon in the marksman's sights.

The toll of terrorism is sporadic rather than large-scale. There have been at least 500 assassinations and more than 60 kidnappings. Hundreds of Spanish and Basque civilians have been killed or injured.

Anti-terrorist measures by the Madrid government have varied from the harsh punishments of Franco's Spain to the less effective blow-hot, blow-cold policies of democratic Spain since 1975. There was a ceasefire in each of the years 1999, 2000 and 2001, then they petered out with little sign that either side took them seriously. Of course, any democratic government working within constitutional limits has to balance along that fine line of acting too severely or too inconsistently. Most Basques declare that they can handle their own home-made terrorism rather than have to depend upon Madrid. Losses have been sustained by ETA – 100 of them have been killed and 20,000 are jailed in Spain or France. Not all Basques are happy with security operations involving Spain and the French.

Effective counter-terrorist work naturally rests on a firm public response. Admittedly, such a show of public resolve by Basques is not likely to match that of Germany two decades ago, as the last chapter described. There is every sign that most Basques are unhappy and bemused by the persistence of something that is inimical to their settled progress and also a major irritant in the eyes of neighbouring Spain. The pointlessness of the terror must be widely realised yet the security forces meet a common reluctance to cooperate and to pass on information. This attitude can hardly be a complacent one. It is as though terrorism has anaesthetised sections of the community. A similar public response, or lack of it, has been noticed in Argentina, Peru and Colombia, save that there ruthless counter-terrorism has led to popular cynicism about violence breeding violence. This cannot be true of the Basque situation.

Terrorism among the Basques is of the 'oddball' variety. Rather as in Northern Ireland, and, to some extent, as in Sri Lanka, terrorist leaders quarrel openly. Like those in Belfast, they find it difficult to 'decommission' their weaponry. Public agitation for peace means wholesale erosion of support. Liberation has been achieved but terrorism rolls on without too obvious a set of objectives.

The IRA in Northern Ireland

Terrorism associated with the Irish Republican Army is yet another variant on a theme. In the year 2003, Northern Ireland is relatively quiet. Terrorism which devastated mind and body in the Province is in a state of suspense. Is it, though, peace at last (there was a peace agreement in April 1998) or is it still war? Those who stand by the Catholic civil movement of Sinn Fein, allied with the IRA, will acknowledge that deep historical roots, the memory and the myth of their struggle for freedom necessitate a readiness to use arms; those on the other Protestant side affirm that the Catholics are in a time warp of their own, making lasting peace uncertain and rendering their own defensive, armed stance an unreasonable one. In the midst of a scarcely reconciled ceasefire and an attempt to fashion partnership in government, each party affirms that Right is on their side. The confrontation is, after all, nearly 100 years old.

In outline, the history of Ireland has always been one of external domination and internal resentment. For over 700 years, the invaders have been Normans and Vikings – each with a capital in Dublin, Tudor knights, Stuart kings, Cromwell's New Model Army, and William of Orange ruthlessly establishing Protestant oligarchy. If in Irish eyes the English have always been the problem, London for the last two centuries has wrestled with the Irish Troubles with very little understanding. The First World War turned Irish nationalism into rejectionist mode and armed it with rifles and high explosive. The British Government, now calling Irish nationalist campaigning 'terrorist', sent battalions of soldiers into a no-win and no-lose situation which has soured relations between London, Dublin and Belfast ever since. It has done nothing to douse a violence potential. There have been concessions – Dublin self-government in 1920 and in 1922 a partition giving the south an Irish Free State of 26 counties and in the north six counties to Belfast and its province of Ulster. Ever since those times, the Nationalist or Republican Catholics of the south (living under a name-change of Eire, and then Ireland) have held themselves apart from Ulster where Unionist Protestants have held dear the link with London and as execrable any notion of unification with the south. An added complication, and a spur to violence, is the existence within Ulster of a Catholic minority vociferous in condemning their second citizen status.

Many years of strife have drawn up the battle lines in three areas of contest: socio-economic, demanding equality between Catholic and Protestant; nationalistic, across the north–south divide; and politico-military, sectarian conflict over barricades. Terror has stalked in many directions, has waxed and waned, and, to the dismay of outsiders, appears to have been given religious blessing.

Serious violence in Ireland has brought convulsion in five phases:

- *1919–39*: IRA formed in 1919 as a commando unit, actively harassing the British in the south and Unionists in the north. Sporadic small-bomb incidents in England. IRA outlawed in 1931 and 1935.
- *1960s*: after being relatively quiet during the Second World War, politico-religious feelings erupted into serious communal rioting in the north, particularly in Belfast and Londonderry. Barricade confrontations between mainly Catholic rioters and 20,000 British Army, and 8,000 armed Royal Ulster Constabulary (RUC). Petrol bombs, victimisation, arson, vigilante 'punishment' squads. Violence now regarded by London as 'terrorist' in the 'worst year', 1969.
- *1970s*: internment of 'terrorists', IRA hunger strikes and martyrdom. Atrocities on all sides. Direct rule imposed 1974. General feelings of civilised breakdown, mob rule, 'no-go areas', inarticulate claims of the violent.
- *1980s*: havoc continues but first signs of rival parties exploring compromises. Large-scale bombing in Ulster and England. Paramilitary units resort to terror tactics. Groundswell of public opinion condemning atrocities clearly influences the 'hard men' among IRA and Unionists.
- *1990s*: signs of terror tactics being discounted, as all sides acknowledge they underestimated the determination of others and overestimated their own capacities. First ceasefire 1994.

The tally of terrorism by the end of the 1990s was 3,500 civilians killed, 30,000 injured and millions of pounds worth of damage to property. The RUC had had 300 officers killed and 9,000 wounded.

A final negotiating position was carved out by 1998 with the so-called Good Friday Agreement ensuring the rights of all through shared Assembly partnership, ongoing day-to-day communal liaison, a Bill of Rights, and prisoner release. There were twin cores in this negotiation, which all contestants at length accepted, namely, that talks would never succeed unless violence was repudiated and, secondly, that all weaponry must be 'decommissioned'.

Five years after 1998 there is a ceasefire and a very obvious public longing for peace. Tension remains and there are occasional incidents. That the Good Friday Agreement is not solidly realisable seems a consequence of several things which have not completely disarmed those termed terrorist. On the Catholic side, there are the long memories of struggle for emancipation and an end to discrimination, the mystique of 'victimhood' and justified (if not sanctified) sacrifice. For many there, it has been said, 'the past is never past – it blinds the perspectives of the present'. Unionists have their past, too, with a bond to Protestantism in England and their 'loyalism' to an English crown. The old slogan of 'No popery', in more modern terms, might be 'No union with Dublin'. Then, there is the problem of disarming. Would we walk naked into negotiation? Neither the past nor the present would forgive us if we did that. Of course, disarmament must displace terror. Everybody realises that. The problem is to decide just how much is to be *our* disarmament – and how much will be *theirs*.

The irony of peace-in-pieces remains. There is progress towards a civilised normality. One last point, however, is disconcerting. The old terrorist brigade of the IRA has split asunder. Inflammable elements are these: the Real IRA, the Continuity IRA, the Dissident IRA and the Official IRA. On the Protestant Unionist flank there are at least six identifiable groups. If terrorism, as it were, is under wraps, there is always the chance of some incident or grudge relighting the flames.

4 Terrorists and their motivation

Earlier chapters have been concerned with a definition of terrorism and they have gone on to survey its dispersion and scale. In the process a number of terrorist motives will have seemed fairly clear. This chapter, though, will look at the issue of motivation in closer detail.

An observer standing beside the steaming wreckage of a bombed hotel or dodging a flurry of police and ambulance crew is bound to wonder what has given rise to mayhem. This chapter will deal with a number of commonly asked questions and there will be an attempt to suggest some answers. Inevitably, there is surmise as to the circumstances, the preconditions, that encourage resort to violence. What possible motives lead the terrorist to prefer carnage to civilised discussion? Are terrorists abnormal, inhuman, even insane? Can assassination, car-bombing, hijacking really be planned in detail by rational people? Terrorists usually belong to groups – what do we know about group motivation? If it is thought that terrorist motives have been established by some forensic means, what is the next stage? Often throwing light upon possible reasons for terrorism leads to heavy condemnation. Is that the end of the matter? Or is it the beginning, if we can then use what we know or suspect of terrorist intentions as a means of dealing with the perpetrators?

Framing tentative answers to tentative questions calls for caution in a number of respects:

- Generally, in the media, the stress on consequences obscures a search for meaning. Careful scrutiny of 'reasons why' will not be easy nor must it be thought of as excusing terrorist motives.

- Much of the search for causation will be based on conjectures and second guessing. Proof will seldom be available.
- The perspectives adopted may affect our judgement – whether we are onlooker, institutional representative, victim or in some way related to a victim.
- Generalisations, perhaps hunches, are likely to disappoint the serious student given the varied contexts in which incidents happen.
- Conclusions about causal factors are frequently simplistic.
- The *cri de cœur* of a terrorist may not be dependable evidence of intent. (Few terrorists agree to be interviewed nor do they commit much to paper.)
- The frequent controversies within terrorist groups may clearly change the nature of motivation and its consistency.
- Terrorist leadership seems notoriously sensitive to change and internal and outside influences. Tracing motivational paths within a group is likely to be quite difficult.

The push into violence

Commonly accepted definitions of terrorist action provide a base for considering the reasons why there is a resort to political violence. They assume that political violence has explicit intentions driving it. It is premeditated, relies on careful strategies and thought-out tactics and is frequently clandestine. Goals, targets, resources, means, risks and exits are calculated. Where violence is indiscriminate others label it terrorist. It may make little difference to condemnation as to whether the incidents are planned or accidental. Motives are to instil fear and uncertainty, to achieve maximum publicity for explicit aims. In the view of Crenshaw, protest pushed into violence is the consequence of two arousing factors, that of *preconditions*, or circumstances which encourage an incentive to resort to violence, and *events* which precipitate violent action (Crenshaw 1981: 381–5).

The nature of motives

Motivation has long been studied by sociologists and psychologists in great detail. Motives can be said to be forces which impel action to realise desires, wants and goals. They may also seek to repel unwanted, threatening or damaging conditions. Motives initiate, direct and sustain behaviour. When considered calmly and rationally, one's motives are liable to sudden or eventual change. For leaders of a group or a movement, motives must be proclaimed to make intentions clear to acolytes and to a wider audience, even to those who will contest intention and goals. Motives are sharp-ended impulses, for example:

- to *acquire* what is unfairly denied – land, freedom, basic rights, opportunities;
- to *reassert* identity, status, legitimate possession, where these are challenged or lost;
- to *protect* where an entity is threatened or ill-treated;
- to *restore* where former rights, privileges, advantages have been denuded or taken away.

Motives on these lines lead to an individual standing up and acting. Such strength of feeling must be shared and the motive becomes a collective one. A vigorous standpoint demands consensus, mobilisation and preparedness to fight in the streets. There is 'no other way'. Viewed as defiance by authority, motives crystallise into determined action. There is always the risk that action pushed over the edge into terror methods is condemned by everyone else.

Political scientists speak of a hierarchy of motives that are multidimensional and likely to change from time to time. Of course, one has to remember that we infer motives from what is said, or written – or even not said. At base level there are values, purposes and aspirations relating to security, and to the autonomy of a political or ethnic group. These are causes to fight for and to die for. More broadly there is a need to protect the well-being of citizens and to preserve political, social, religious and cultural institutions. These are core objectives. A prime motive, at all times, is to struggle to realise them by any and all means. Middle-range objectives, secondary motives – the promotion of esteemed values at home and abroad, the retrieval of deserved prestige, the creation of fairer opportunities, the securing of allies and friends, the progressive weakening of opponents – they will necessitate commitment to a longer struggle which may involve a drip-by-drip harrowing of an oppressor. There is a long-term vision of objectives which when fully realised will legitimate a struggle, however intense and destructive. Full self-determination, and inter-national recognition of status, are the ultimate objectives for which motives have to be strong on confidence and hope. Ever present, though, is the troublesome thought that protest pushed into violence may achieve something yet delay or prevent attainment.

One can think of the core objectives that were defended at barri-cades in Belfast and Londonderry, that inspired blacks in apartheid South Africa, that still feed the clamorous protestations of Palestinian Arabs. Tamils blaze away at a Sri Lankan government apparently believing that a bloody securing of core objectives will enable them to move further up the hierarchy. Climbing up that ladder is likely to cost lives by the thousand. In Sri Lanka, in Northern Ireland and among the Basques, the middle-range and long-term objectives and the motives that reach for them are consistently stated.

In the Middle East a range of motives can be discerned oper-ating at a number of distinct levels. Fundamentally, the mainspring for the Palestinian Arab living under Israeli subjection is to work for its overthrow. He will do this by means of active resistance to any Jewish occupation or edict. Younger Arabs will join the *intifada* (uprising), older ones will lend their shoulders to any group effort to demonstrate and interfere with Tel Aviv's sense of order. Today is what matters: the mid-range and distant future objectives are worth waiting for. Certain Palestinians have no truck with waiting. The savage demands of the crusading *jihad* recog-nise no limits to motives and methods – they are apocalyptic in Western eyes. The suicide bomber, the car bomber, the sniper, wrench lives out of opposers, and of anyone who gets in the way. Here the main urge is primitive. In recent years, evident splits have been visible between more moderate Arab leadership and opinion and *fedayeen* commandos such as Hizbullah, Hamas and the Democratic Front for Palestine. The moderate wing fears that continued suicide bombing by the Palestinians' religious fanatics only plays into the hands of Ariel Sharon and his militarists. Motives are misdirected. Political urgency has been accompanied by religious imperatives which assert that the blessed state of martyrdom is a matchless motive.

Again, in the Middle East, there are those that Israel lambasts as proto-terrorists. They are professional people, doctors, lawyers, teachers, journalists and many businessmen. For them the prime motive is to back all three objectives, core, medium-term and long-term, indirectly. They will not engage in face-to-face confrontations and violence nor align themselves with the backwardness of Islamic fundamentalists. Vigorous support is lent to their more active brethren in the field and certainly generous funds are contributed. It is quite possible that terrorist coffers benefit from some of this money unbeknown to sponsors. Muslims such as these feel committed to defending Islam against infidel intervention (with the United States as the chief enemy) and, more long-term, they are concerned to root out corruption, heresy and injustice in such places as Saudi Arabia, Kuwait, Bahrain, places tainted by Western materialism. One in four international terrorist incidents is located in the Middle East. It is, indeed, a tragedy that this and other factors lead so many people to characterise the inhabitants of that region as predisposed to violence, willing members of freelance terrorist groups operating in host countries or state-sponsored ones where the major motive is seen as visceral antipathy towards the non-Muslim world. This generalisation is a harmful one. Terrorists, the world over, are what one might term a slender rejectionist minority.

A mention should be made of the threat of violence from the extreme right. The post-war world has had to contend with neo-fascist and neo-Nazi groups in Germany, France, Italy, Russia, the United States, Canada, South Africa and South America. There have been electoral gains and a worrying rash of racist attacks in many countries. Motives represent dogged, ill-informed prejudice which is hard to meet since much of it relies on orchestrated street brawls and fiery publications and meetings. A number of countries such as Britain have legislation to deal with this upsurge, which is regarded chiefly as a domestic scourge rather than an international one.

Lastly, there is the incidence of issue-specific terrorism where the aim is to change particular practices or policies, not the political system. The authorities are quick to label such demonstrations as 'terrorist' whether it is a group of animal rights followers burning down a laboratory practising vivisection, or a task force of the Green Party destroying acres of a genetically modified crop. In the United States, 'anti-abortionist' violence has given scientific discussion a very bad name. There is a large moral issue here for debate. How far, in a democracy, may civil protest be allowed expression before it is understood to 'overstep the bounds'? Is it legitimate to disrupt a world conference if the disrupters rely on significant violence? What are the criminal implications of 'the committed' wrecking computer links and contaminating commercial products? To what extent should government or a local authority stand back if lives and property are endangered? The best of motives may turn out to be hazardous to community well-being.

Precipitating events

Nobody would claim that any one event necessarily triggers violence in a community. However, it does seem that where tension is pronounced then a single incident or a string of events may constitute 'the last straw' for those whose political activism is vibrant and frustrated. An example of this is in West Germany in the 1960s (referred to in Chapter 2), when students particularly felt the impulse to stand and declare stridently that there was a need for urgent reform in the constitution and in the universities. When their impulses steered them into street demonstrations they met fierce riot control measures. Police truncheons clubbed and killed a Berlin student protesting at the visit of the Shah of Iran in June 1967. Outraged beyond endurance, the original motive of peaceful protest and insistence was transformed into something so compelling to others that an estimated 60,000 students and trade unionists marched against something they termed 'closet Nazism'.

There were a number of leaders who gave shape to the deepening agitation in the 1970s. Rudi Dutschke, Ulrike Meinhof, Andreas Baader, Gudrun Enslinn wrote broadsheets, to be distributed in thousands, calling for 'subversive action – at all costs'. Destructive action was more potent than preaching. Revolutionary cells would carry further an 'armed struggle'. Arson and bombs ravaged town centres. The motive now was 'Destroy that which is destroying you'. At the same time, too, links were forged with like-minded practitioners of terror in Belgium, Greece, Libya and Syria. The committed were now ready to kill.

Interestingly, there is evidence of the German terrorists' motivation in five volumes of analysis compiled by the West German government in the mid-1980s (Merkl, in Crenshaw 1995: 176–8).

Most of the terrorists came from white-collar families. Half of them were from broken families and one in three was female. These conflict-ridden youths do appear to have had difficulty with their perspectives and rationality. In their verbal conflicts (usually when arrested) they struck their interviewers as excessively dogmatic and hyper-emotional. Their political judgements were black-and-white, crude and ill-informed. Motives were impulsive and inconsistent. Within a year or two, and especially if they had been arrested and charged, a quarter of the young terrorists had abandoned the terror enterprise. It had been a protest generation between 1967 and 1991, mixed in membership, allegiance and motive. Its end was as much due to internal confusion and irresolution as to sustained hammering by the security services and a growing disinclination by the German public to be blackmailed by sporadic violence.

Contemporary terrorists move through a similar process to the German generation in response to incidents which strike them as challenging and abhorrent. Ulster's Catholics cannot forget the Dublin riots of 1915. Of that time it has been said that there was an angry alliance of idealists within the Sinn Fein nationalist movement who were imbued with romantic notions of Celtic revival, together with armed militiamen mustering armed force. England's past excesses, the continuing prevarication from London against Irish self-rule and the prospect of English curbs on future Irish progress were not so much dreams as motivating forces pushing the Irish towards complete independence. Part-religious, part-political memories are at the root of more recent anguish over inflammatory incidents such as the peremptory sacking of Catholic shop stewards in the Belfast Harland and Wolff shipyard, and the refusal of appeals against summary arrest and eviction of Catholic 'troublemakers' from housing estates in Londonderry. Nationalists in the IRA regarded this as a basic challenge and their core motive was to respond with fire. It is disconcerting that, although the 1998 Peace Agreement has brought five years of peace, the sectarian divide remains visible with the forces on each side of the divide fragmented into smaller groups, armed still and each quietly nursing a readiness to spring into action should the mood call for it.

Motivation and context

Definition of terrorism is only really intelligible, according to Crenshaw, if the enfolding contexts of time and place are taken into account. That must be true when motives are scrutinised. A brief consideration of motivation among contemporary terrorist groups will help to make the point clearer.

Europe has to take account of terrorists motivated by deeply-felt separatist intentions as is illustrated in Northern Ireland, Chechnya, Bosnia, Georgia, Nagorno-Karabakh and the Basque ETA movement. Campaigning is low-cost, sometimes spasmodic, and public sympathies cannot always be assured.

African terrorism has been most pronounced in the central republic of Rwanda. Armed militias from rival tribes, the Tutsi and the Hutu, have set out systematically to hunt down and eliminate others on a vast scale. Typically, this terror warring is savage and without compromise. Whole sectors of a civilian population are often terrorised into fleeing their homes to escape genocidal massacre, rape and torture as in 'ethnic cleansing'.

South-east Asia, as noted earlier, so dependent upon capitalist intervention from outside, longs to throw it off. This struggle is a mix of neo-Marxist notions and Islamic faith. Indonesia has its 'dark forces' of rogue ex-soldiers and others, almost certainly with al-Qaida mercenaries, who are willing to wreck the economy and bring down the government, as the Bali bomb showed in October 2002. Ironically, the government in the capital, Jakarta, has had to enrol more outside interventionism, in the shape of a Special Forces task squad from the United States. In nearby Pakistan, still a sanctuary for al-Qaida and the defeated Taliban, the mainsprings of terrorism are more overtly political, stimulated with a murderous urge to destroy any trace of United States influence. Pakistan looks nervously at Afghanistan where warlords enrol their own bands of desperate tribesmen, armed to the teeth and ready to kill by order. Motives here are raw – mercenary, political, religious (without much asceticism or piety) and on the whole entirely destructive. In Kashmir, for so many years the contest ring between India and Pakistan, each of the major states accuses the other of sponsoring terrorists to fight the cause of separatism. (In the background is the thought that these two governments, which harshly accuse each other of violent conspiracy, are nuclear powers.)

Japan has had to cope with a serious terrorist group, the Aum Shinrikyo, the 'Supreme Truth'. These zealots, led by a half-blind mystic, Shoko Asahara, planned in 1995 to kill Tokyo commuters by injecting a nerve gas, Sarin, into the air-shafts of the capital's underground railway system. Their Buddhist and Shinto beliefs were allied with disgust at the rottenness and technocratic obsessions of contemporary Japan. A cataclysmic event, some sort of Big Bang, would usher in heaven on earth. It was never entirely clear whether Ahara's disciples were waiting for disaster to strike or whether they were working hard with the motive of bringing it about. Gas clouds on a March morning in 1995 asphyxiated 5,000 travellers and killed a dozen of them. Intensive investigations took nine months and then the Aum's leader and close associates were arrested and accused of mass murder. Japan and the rest of the world are still pondering the chances of a similar incident using, say, nuclear or radiological materials, to bring about an Armageddon.

There is a more complex set of motives in Central and South America. In Argentina, Peru, Guatemala and Honduras there are elements of the extreme left dedicated to Marxist diffusion and to the toppling of any regime they deem capitalist and repressive. Frustration drives many into violence, sometimes that of the urban guerrilla. Colombia has the added scourge of virulent gang warfare occasioned by rivalry over narcotics trading, where competitive urge may lead to a cut throat.

An intriguing example of motivational change in South America is the case of Peru. Nobody could ever have thought that a group of young professors in a rural university would ever launch a vicious reign of terror. Originally, in 1963, they set out to rein-vigorate poor Indian villages with welfare work and skills training. Although among the academics there were Maoists and Marxists, they were able to work fruitfully with the Peruvian government. After a promising start, the project's initiators became convinced that only a wholesale transformation of both government and society could benefit the peasantry. Motives were turning rigid and sour.

By the mid-1970s the government in Lima had grown under-standably fearful. Their tentative control measures only embold-ened the professors. The educational programme, the Shining Path to the Future, the way of peace, now became the Shining Path

(Sendero Luminoso), the way of terrorism and a people's war. Motives and methods were now completely and ominously different. Regional committees recruited almost 10,000 people, dispersing them across the countryside in guerrilla cells. Shining Path had turned itself into a terrorist group with their original leader, Professor Guzman, as a megalomaniac messiah. Motives had swerved sideways into eliminating anyone who was not a party member. Power for the people had hideously become power for the party. Thirty thousand lives have been lost in Peru. Two thousand five hundred terrorists have been arrested, together with Guzman. There remain, though, perhaps 200 in the shadows, armed and active in crime and narcotics dealing. Once again, terrorist motives lie in suspense.

It is often thought that the pressures of existence within urban communities give rise to promptings which call for a violent outlet. The West Bank of the River Jordan in Israel could certainly provide some substance for this idea. Half of the population there is under the age of 15. Two out of three of these are jobless, 70 per cent of them drop out of school, 50 per cent rely on welfare 'dole' for income. Their helplessness and revolt swelled after December 1987 into defiance when a watching world saw youths pelting the Israeli Defence Force with rocks and petrol bombs. For them there can have been no alternative spur and gesture. There was, though, a bewitching political imperative, Death to Israel. Elsewhere, in the megacities of the New World or Asia, disadvantage, discrimination, poverty and decay reach an epidemic scale. Terrorism, though, is not endemic. Undoubtedly, the absence of a strong and consistent political input turns destructive impulses into street crime.

The rationality of the terrorist

Trauma usually breeds prompt decision. Those who have carved out a path of violence are thought to be inhuman and insane. Can their motives be calculated and rational? If it is possible to work out their possible motives are these not so inexcusable that retaliation seems an appropriate response? However, terrorists these days are generally considered to be rational in beliefs and behaviour. They certainly claim to be so. Readers will recall, after all, that a widely accepted definition of terrorism is that it is a premeditated threat or use of violence intended to intimidate. From time to time random and impulsive acts of destruction hit the headlines but the evidence reveals that individuals, generally members of groups, estimate carefully the risks involved in carrying out their strategies. They think carefully about objectives, perhaps compiling a list of them. Feasible targets are selected and options taken into account. Detailed planning goes into tactics. Where and when will it be best to act? How many people will be needed? What methods are to be used? How do we set about the business? Who will be chosen for particular tasks? What about the security of the place we intend to attack? And how do we get away afterwards, that is, unless we have a suicide mission in mind?

It came as a shock to many people to realise that the 19 well-educated terrorists responsible for 9/11 had been training for three years with the hijacking and crashing of four aircraft in mind. Their plans were meticulously drafted. Yet, how rational were these men? One might argue that terrorists of this ilk associate political calculations with destructive and symbolic expressions of contempt and hatred and that in so doing their rational decisions have more to do with their thinking out, point by point, appropriate means to secure particular goals.

Motives originating as political or ideological or religious are soon translated into compulsive ideas and behaviour. These are not necessarily resulting in violence. Quite often the terrorist who does not wish to be so labelled will point out that violence was not of his choosing – it was the unreasonableness and hostility of the opposition. A minority of people will find intolerable the prejudice and hostility of a majority, as has been the case for Muslims in the Balkans or for Cypriot Turks. In many South American countries a blinding lack of opportunity both for workers and intellectuals has pushed them into radical and ultimately violent groups. Protest has got them nowhere against the brutality of the police or army: only their own force will prevail, and that leads to risks and suffering. For youth, unsuccessful and rebellious, an urge to kick back may go further than individual deviance to enrolling in an armed brigade of fellow-sufferers. To be a member of an action gang is a powerful motive and most terrorist gangs find little difficulty in recruiting angry young men and women. They yearn for action, for praise from leaders and peers, for the oxygen of publicity.

Motives in the group

Speculation about the mindset and motives of the terrorist covers a realm of print. Not many definite conclusions have been reached, for, after all, terrorists have shown no liking for recorded interview or the psychiatrist's couch. It is clear that the causes of terrorism lie within the individual, the group he or she joins, and the nature of society at large.

What sort of people turn into terrorists? Facts are scarce but some rather hypothetical sketch of personality has frequently been possible. Peer pressure, chance encounters, perhaps imitative behaviour, appear to draw in adolescents, sometimes from broken families, whose lives hitherto have lacked success. They may feel alienated, distanced from opportunity, perhaps exploited, and altogether marginalised in the community. Adolescence for many is a time of rebellion against established values and authority in home and society. Deeper difficulties with self-confidence and self-image trouble many young people.

Research has shown that terrorists, in general, are normal people, neither psychopaths nor mentally deranged (Reich 1998: 224, 269). The terrorist, one could say, is 'action-orientated', aggressive, keen to find excitement, with a fair measure of intolerance and readiness to find fault with others but not necessarily violent by nature. Those coming from the margins of society realise for the first time in life that they really belong to something. What matters is what you feel called upon to do now. The others, after all, are doing the same. Nor is there any compunction to search within yourself for the explanation of earlier failures. Unwilling or unable to face up to self-scrutiny, the terrorist easily blames others in 'the establishment'. Scapegoats will be found. Anger may turn into hatred and explosive violence.

Evidently, the members of a terrorist group are liable to changes in behaviour once they join. The sociologist W. R. Bion, in 1961, has described how the group member is led to submerge individual identity, the more readily to take on board a group's rules, motives and moral code (Reich 1998: 31–2). An individual, in belonging to a group or gang, is offered an opportunity for action and in so doing falls in with the dictates of his leader and fellow members. Bion, in a study of group dynamics, has the leader as arbiter of motives and consequences. Deliberately weighing risks and odds, he may detail the group to adopt either 'fight' or 'flight' tactics. In the event of fighting, the recruits will accept his decision as to ways and means, targets and timing. No member is likely to show disloyalty, risking their membership and the disapproval (if not worse) of the leader. Committed to certain goals and methods, the leader, the recruit and the rest must show iron-bound consensus. In this light, violence is easy enough to accept even by those who would never have chosen it by themselves.

Before long, no member of a group will dare to cut the strings of attachment. Withdrawal becomes quite impossible, in the view of Jerrold M. Post, an American research psychiatrist (Post, in Reich 1998: 25–40). Values and moral codes that were learned before joining the group fade away. Motives for terrorist attack which once would have horrified the recruit are now feasible and pardonable. The leader has pronounced them, the others in the group have sanctioned them. Post quotes an example of this from the German group, the Red Army Faction, where a young recruit, told of the plan to burn down a department store, protests that this will lead to the loss of innocent lives. The reaction from his fellows was ice-cold as they grimly questioned his motives and dependability. At all costs, recruits and group will go on for the sake of the cause and the very existence of a dedicated number. Survival is an absolute priority. Whatever the degree of risk, the group will continue to terrorise. There can be no compromise.

How does anybody outside a group of terrorists help in its disbandment? There are possibilities, according to Jerrold Post. For a start, we might think of reasons why a particular terrorist feels so alienated and inadequate that he finds the allurement of a terrorist group irresistible.

Very carefully, alternative 'paths out' must be provided by way of dissuasion and to facilitate breaking away from the old allegiance. An approach such as this has been tried experimentally in Northern Ireland where stalwart members of the IRA have been released from the Maze Prison to be promised the security of an amnesty, help with relocation, tangible welfare benefits and reliable job opportunities. It has not been easy, in a Northern Ireland almost wrecked by its sectarian feuding, to guarantee public understanding of a need to rehabilitate the terrorist and reshape his motives.

Terrorist motives are essentially two-headed. There is the initial destructive impulse of he who would create a paralysing sense of fear in a target community. There is another impulse quite different from that behind the launching of a conventional military attack. The terrorist's arsenal is one of psychological warfare. Motives use the imagination of others, either directly or through the media. Anxiety and uncertainty are manipulated so that a victim or an onlooker helps the terrorist to achieve his ends. The terrified, pressuring the establishment, are the helpmates of the terrorist.

5   Three terrorist profiles

What sort of person may become a terrorist? Profiles of a number of notorious terrorists tell us something of their personalities and inclinations. The exercise needs care, though, since an incident is deemed an outrage and there follows a flurry of speculation in the media and, all too often, a degree of misrepresentation of what psychiatrists and other authorities have tentatively pronounced. In the light of these reservations, this chapter guardedly offers several profiles compiled from the evidence there is on hand:

1   Timothy McVeigh convicted of the Oklahoma City bombing of April 1995 (*Washington Post*, 2 July 1995).
2   Theodore Kaczynski, the 'Unabomber' in the United States, also of 1995 (*CNN*, 1997).
3   Osama bin Laden, mainly since 1992 (International Policy Institute for Counter-terrorism [Bodansky 2001: *passim*; Williams 2002: *passim*]).

Timothy McVeigh

In many respects, the young McVeigh (born in 1968) conforms to a stereotype of an angry young man. He came from a broken family in a downtown part of New York State. Reasonably bright at school, he became uninterested in college and a further career and soon succumbed to pronounced feelings of alienation. Fending for himself was getting him nowhere and society was letting him down at every turn. Seen by those who knew him as 'unexceptional' and 'frankly nondescript', he found some recognition as a gun club enthusiast, spending lonely hours shooting at targets in the backwoods. His gun skills soon gained him membership of a fringe cult of disaffected youth who, styling themselves as American Patriots, were secretly concerned to oppose government restrictions on their 'freedom' to bear arms. From time to time McVeigh would be among an armbanded squad marching down Main Street, frequently to the derision of passers-by. Already, in his late teens, McVeigh was feeling the certainty that it was not so much a patriot conspiracy as a federal one directed at such as him. Furthermore, he was hearing every day of the resentment of neighbouring blue-collar workers in a car assembly plant. Washington had no regard for the common man.

McVeigh's frustrations soon moved into fantasy. As he confessed later, there were the beginnings of an apocalyptic drive to bring down a repressive federal authority. Fighting the government meant defending oneself. Aged 20, he spent his savings as a fast food salesman on buying a small parcel of land. Here he was to build a semi-underground survivalist bunker, light it with a rudimentary generator, and stock it with tinned food and potable water. The logistics of McVeigh's War were carefully planned.

The United States Army was to give McVeigh the further weapons competence that would suit his need for defensiveness. As an enlisted soldier he made excellent progress and was soon made a sergeant in a tough unit. He made a good friend in Terry Nichols, an older GI, and one later to be an accomplice in the Oklahoma City bombing. Fellow members of his corps saw him as cold, calculating and rather obsessive – in turn he fulminated against the White House, Communist fellow-travellers, Jews and blacks. November 1990 gave him the chance of action and recognition in a drafting to the Gulf War. That engagement was short, sharp and, in a sense, rewarding, for McVeigh was decorated for bravery and initiative.

His next step seems out of character. The violence he had met, not only in the front line but back at a Special Forces base, now upset him. The soldiers around him were clearly 'sickos'. The army, too, was upset on account of the sergeant's aimless frustration – discharge was the only solution. The *Washington Post*, writing in retrospect, was in little doubt about the significance of McVeigh's moves at this point. The recruit was to become a renegade. It was the beginning of 'An ordinary boy's extraordinary rage'.

As a security guard at a defence contractor's plant in 1991, McVeigh was able to hone his capacities for surveillance and method taking. More than ever it was the tyranny of governmental intrusion that threatened his way of life, indeed, his very survival. He wrote to a local paper in heated, anguished terms: 'America is in serious decline and I am too. Do we have to shed blood to reform the present system? I hope not – but it might be so'.

Two years later, in April 1993, and in an attempt to restrain a fundamentalist religious sect, the Branch Davidians, from violence, a sortie by the FBI went drastically wrong. Eighty disciples perished in a blazing inferno in their citadel in Waco, Texas, with no chance of escape. For McVeigh this was a government attack and an atrocity. Waco must be avenged. Violence to oust violence must in turn be smashed.

Timothy McVeigh, so he said, moved into his 'action phase'. This might mean martyrdom for a desperate man who knew he alone was right. He was, he later admitted, in a state of 'siege'. The final act was to pile explosives into a van and to send it on its way into the Alfred P. Murragh Federal Building in the centre of Oklahoma City. America has never forgotten the horror of the morning of 21 April 1995, the loss of 168 office workers, 19 children and more than 400 injured.

Timothy McVeigh, not far from the explosion scene, was, in fact, pulled up for a traffic offence. Interviewed for that, down at police headquarters, the actual terrorist could not forbear to talk openly about what had occurred. Of course, he regretted the 'collateral damage' of innocent lives lost, but for him it was a small price to pay for striking a blow at a great institution. Inevitably, McVeigh would be subjected to a long process of investigation and judicial arraignment as a bombing suspect.

The trial of McVeigh, and, now, of a suspected co-terrorist, Terry Nichols, was moved to Denver to ensure a fairer trial location. In June 1997 McVeigh was found guilty on 11 counts of first degree murder and conspiracy, to be dealt with by capital punishment. Nichols, seen as prime accomplice, received a life sentence. The prosecuting attorney's last words summarised an even wider verdict on the terrorists. 'The [bomb] truck', he said, 'was there to impose the will of Timothy McVeigh on the rest of America and to do so by premeditated violence and terror'. The rest of America was stunned to realise that the arch-terrorist was not a plotter from east of Suez but a young Middle American, with a bland sense of American self-composure.

It was expected that the most wanted man in America would appeal. Not until January 1998, three years after the bombing, did McVeigh's lawyers call for a retrial, believing that prejudice, emotion, hearsay and the defendant's own confusion and contradictions had invalidated the legal process. Twelve months of courtroom wrangling and a good deal of public protest sank the appeal effort, more especially on account of the accused's unpreparedness to appeal. More than that, he longed for death, wanting 'one that will be seen on prime time TV'. McVeigh was executed in June 2001 – in the eyes of many, a very public martyr.

Theodore Kaczynski – The 'Unabomber'

The 'Unabomber' was an acronym used by the United States FBI to refer to the mysterious serial killer they had been hunting for 18 years between 1978 and 1995. Someone, somewhere was posting letters or small packets containing home-made explosives to the homes of university professors or business executives in airline companies. Unsealing the envelope or undoing the parcel would have lethal consequences. Already, 3 people had been killed and 29 injured. Target recipients appeared to have been selected at random and there had been 16 attacks. Laboratory workers in the FBI spent countless, fruitless hours trying to piece together an elaborate jigsaw.

In the event, the killer-terrorist was his own undoing. In the summer of 1995 the *New York Times* and the *Washington Post* each received in the post, not a bomb, but a 35,000-word manuscript entitled Industrial Society and its Future. The whole manuscript was a devastating criticism of modern industrialism and its despoliation of the environment. The newspaper editors also received the strangest of assurances in an accompanying letter, namely, that if the newspapers published this manifesto then the author would call off the bomb-in-the-mail campaign. It looked like a literal rendering of the old maxim 'publish or be damned'. Editors concluded that it would be best to publish with a reference to the author's threat and at the same time contact the FBI. A frustrated security force was delighted, for their forensic methods had got them nowhere. Coincidentally, and some months later, a young man, David Kaczynski, turning out his mother's attic, was astounded to read up there papers from his older, academic brother, Theodore Kaczynski, which were a mirror image of work in the by now publicised manifesto. Appalled by what he had found, the obvious connection to a terrorist, he too approached the authorities. The arrest of Theodore Kaczynski, a mathematics professor at the University of California's complex at Berkeley, followed. Investigators narrowed down a search for the terrorist's home base to a remote cabin in forested Montana. There they found shelves of scientific books and journals, several typewriters and, most helpfully, blueprints for simple explosive devices together with a half-assembled prototype. These things were the product of a most methodical originator. There were no fingerprints. Serial numbers of batteries used in the bomb kits had been erased. The super-terrorist had never licked stamps to avoid leaving any DNA trace. Most revealing of all was a much-thumbed copy of the manifesto.

Dated September 1995, the manifesto sternly called for an end to industrial technology. Revolution was the ultimate answer rather than piecemeal reform. Otherwise, we remained prisoners of a disastrous, dehumanising system which corrupted the scientist, the manager, personnel in institutions, and the rest of us as consumers and clients. The environment became devastated. Nature's resources were imperilled. All of us are vulnerable against a monstrous technical regime which saps our autonomy and our dignity.

Those who have read Kaczynski's manifesto have not found either the rationale or the sometimes far from lucid style particularly convincing. It is hyper-Ludditism, which may be an allowable point of view even for a scientist who owes much of his training and later research facilities to the advantages of technology. What strikes most readers is the malevolent conclusion that only collapsing the system will confer blessing. 'Until the power of the industrial system has been thoroughly wrecked ... destruction of that system must be the revolutionaries' only goal' – such is the chilling call for action.

There seems to be some resemblance to Timothy McVeigh, apart from the fact that one had nothing much to say and the other had too much to say (oblivious to the dangers with that). Both are confused, uncertain, contradictory, secretive and obsessive.

Both of them seem to have vacillated emotionally from eerie silence in company to outbursts of violent rage. Neither of them found it easy to make any success of relationships with others, both of them were crippled emotionally. Each of them yearned for publicity and, when they achieved that, there was no remorse for what they had done and no admission of doing wrong. When arrested, both men were ready to confess, dramatically and in detail. Each was methodical in planning. In many respects these personality characteristics are what we expect of the terrorist.

Public exposure was a rather theatrical experience for McVeigh and Kaczynski. The Oklahoma bomber relished ample television coverage of his personality and of what he had done. So keen was the Unabomber to interest the public that, when awaiting trial in California in 1997, it was arranged somehow with a New Jersey TV company that a teleconference be set up. A studio was hastily set up in a penal compound and Kaczynski permitted to air his 'ecoterrorism'. Equally unusual in the light of conventional legal process was the failure to insist on full psychiatric examination of the arrested terrorist. This was a point that the presiding judge was to deplore. How, otherwise, could we understand the frame of mind of an accused terrorist? However, although both defence and prosecution would have wanted this, the accused would not participate.

The trial was a lengthy affair dragging on through 1997. The prosecution believed they had a clear case with no shortage of circumstantial evidence and, indeed, plenty of voluntary admission from the man in the dock. Defence attorneys stressed the abnormality of the defendant. He was obviously deranged, a victim of paranoid schizophrenia, as expert opinion was concluding. This would dispose him to rational incapacity in action and judgement. His recourse to terror methods was impulsive, not the calculated design of a power-at-all-costs fanatic. A plea for insanity was offered on the lines of diminished responsibility. The judge accepted the plea of *non compos mentis* and gave Kaczynski a life sentence, in January 1998. At the time there were those in court and outside who could not reconcile the 'lightness' of the sentence with the horrific crimes committed. Surely, and a conventional opinion, the terrorist, as a proved methodical man, must have had those sane moments when he decided the why and the wherefore of mass killing. What continued to puzzle lawyers and the general public was the riddle of why a highly intelligent scientist should think that 'destruction' of an endangering society could be brought about by despatching noxious packages to 30-odd individuals picked out at random.

There is a final bizarre point. The convicted Unabomber continued to write in his prison cell. There was a large public demand for anything he wrote that could be leaked out of prison. Fifteen thousand copies of the manifesto have been sold. Any money earned in consequence went not to the author but as a form of compensation to his victims. There was a short commercial excursion into selling Unabomber T-shirts and posters until the prison governor stopped it. Internet viewers in California could even visit a site set up in 1995, the Una-Pac website, which continued for a time to disseminate non-violent views similar to those of America's most prominent ecoterrorist. Another riddle remains: as a *CNN News* report put it, was Theodore Kaczynski 'an evil man or a tortured soul'?

Osama bin Laden

The third terrorist profile is that of Osama bin Laden. Little known to the general public before the year 2000 or so, he is now demonised in the Western media as the mainspring of a universally-feared terrorist organisation, al-Qaida. His charisma in his native Middle East, his material resources, the conspirators he can call upon, the funds that he can gather, all these are reportedly enormous. This terrorist is alive, the object of endless searches and a flood of speculation. He is pre-eminently different from McVeigh and Kaczynski for he is a leader-extraordinary and a most influential ideologue. He is a tycoon-terrorist.

Osama bin Muhammed bin Laden was born in 1957 in Saudi Arabia's capital, Riyadh, into a family of small-time builders. The oil boom of the 1970s transformed the fortunes of the bin Ladens and they became involved in large-scale construction work all round the Persian Gulf. This brought them great affluence and important connections. Osama was to graduate in economics and management and was expected to join the board of his father's mammoth engineering concern. Remembered by his peers as devoutly religious, as shy and considerate towards others, he did not lack social ease. He was rarely flustered and never quick to anger. Usually ready to size up an opportunity, he already displayed the makings of a leader.

The young economist mixed freely with clerics and individuals in Riyadh who impressed Osama with the need to go out and challenge the heresies, mostly Western in origin, that threatened to corrupt the believer. This would be non-violent protest, although it seems to have occurred to bin Laden, already at this stage, that taking up the challenge would involve a *jihad*, a religious duty to use all possible force to make your way. Almost more at home in the mosque and its cloistered sharia school, bin Laden might have remained an engineer with a strong, rather intellectualised sense of grievance against heretical Muslims and, worse still, against corrupting Western infiltration. He might have stayed essentially a man of peace. Two challenges were to present themselves after 1979 – the Soviet invasion of Afghanistan and, 11 years later, the United States attack on Iraq, the Gulf War. Taking up these challenges turned bin Laden into a man of war.

Ten years of dogged frontline service as leader of an Arab *mujahideen* contingent perfected bin Laden's operational skills and earned him wide respect for helping rout the Soviet infidel. Towards the end of the campaigning, bin Laden established a service centre for the many thousands of young Arabs who had come to assist Afghan liberation. This was known as 'the Base', or al-Qaida, and there may have been in the mind of its founder the possibility of expanding its work both to undergird the fundamentalist Taliban government and, further, to facilitate strong-armed, single-minded missionary work on behalf of a purified and protected Islam. The battle-hardened Saudi veteran and his associates soon envisaged the need to fight on all fronts, against Communism, capitalist countries such as the United States, corrupt Arab dynastic rule and expansionist Israel. There was the shaping here of a powerful, demonic mix of ultra-religious crusade, twisted politics, and the usefulness of a highly-trained and committed band. Fervent 'Afghan Veterans' were deployed to join the Islamic struggles in Bosnia, Kosovo, Chechnya, Somalia, Sudan and Algeria, where conflicts raged in unlimited ferocity. Bin Laden had become a man of terror.

The Gulf War challenge of 1990–1 was decisive in revealing the United States as a prime target for invective and destructive action. Had not 20,000 American troops and squadrons of aircraft violated the sanctity of Islam's holiest of places? Now, bin Laden's feelings of outrage, as it were, primed the gun. He would retreat to Sudan to think, to consult, to plan. In the meantime, his native Saudi Arabia deprived this uncompromising troublemaker of his citizenship.

Sudan became a terrorist workshop after 1992. To take on the West called for a carefully built organisational structure, a network or 'spaghetti' form of management, with cells in perhaps 50 countries. Activists were to be selected, trained and posted. Bin Laden proved a masterful organiser. Engineer, qualified macro-manager, articulate in speech and writing, computer literate, highly informed about politics and religion, he put together something he was convinced as a pragmatic visionary that would reap a whirlwind. There was no trouble in providing funds. Possibly £300 million of his huge personal fortune had accrued from civil engineering schemes, farming projects and some narcotics trading. This would now endow violent political action, or terrorism in most vocabularies. Al-Qaida was now confirmed as the overall name of a meticulously designed, large enterprise. The remit would be to export terrorising strategies and methods to places where oppression reigned in Europe, Africa and Asia. Sleeper cells were established in Teheran, Geneva, Cyprus, Khartoum and Bosnia. Bin Laden travelled widely making new contacts. There was a short spell living in north London.

By 1998 the plans of the super-terrorist were firm and dry. Spectacular demonstrations of intent and powers were now possible and there were bombings directed at American interests in Germany, the Netherlands, Saudi Arabia, Bahrain, Kenya and Tanzania. Governments across the world revealed their anxiety about something they christened Terrorism Incorporated. The initiator, Osama bin Laden, was reviled on all sides as a wicked menace to civilisation. The horrific blasting of the twin towers in New York in 2001 was blamed on al-Qaida and its inspiring head, although that individual did not admit his culpability and any real proof was hard to come by.

Most certainly the attack on Afghanistan following 9/11 was designed by the United States as a 'surgical operation', so it was said, to get rid of al-Qaida and the Taliban government which had given the terrorists sanctuary. Osama bin Laden was reported to have his command centre in a remote cave-bunker, one fitted with the latest sophisticated means of control and communication. United States marines and Cruise missiles were able eventually to bring a fragile peace and order to a pulverised, fratricidal land. Of bin Laden, hunted most carefully, there remains no trace. There is a reward of US$5 million to those who capture this Pimpernel figure.

Rhetoric is a trademark of this terrorist, beamed either from his own studio in a mountain eyrie or through *al-Jazeera*, an Arab broadcasting station. One speech, afterwards made widely available in Arab markets on a videocassette, declared that today's world was split into two camps – 'the camp of the believers and the camp of the unbelievers'. Bin Laden intimated that only an 'environment of terror' would eliminate the 'Satanic unbelievers'. At about the same time, in 2001, President George Bush bisected the world in similar fashion. There were in the Global Village 'those who are with us and those who are against us'. This was perhaps not a helpful statement in view of the Bush anxiety not to stage an East–West conflict and to frame a universal anti-terrorist coalition where, as he said, 'the large majority of the world's people will join in fighting terrorism'.

Bin Laden's immense conviction considers the employment of terror methods as forwarding the cause of Allah. Again, in 2001 this message went out over the internet:

> The time has come for all the world's Muslims, especially the youth, to unite against the apostates and continue a *jihad* until these forces are crushed to naught . . . and wiped from the face of this earth. The time has come for acquiring weapons for the defence of the Muslim's religious duty . . . It would be a sin for Muslims not to try to possess these weapons . . .
>
> (Message received and recorded by
> *Pakistan Daily News*, 19 June 2001)

Sentiments such as these resonate powerfully throughout Islam. They tap into emotive urges and political imperatives derived from hunger for power and hunger for food and water. A mark of Muslim veneration is to be gauged from titles bestowed on the millionaire terrorist. The honour of *emir* confirms him as a religious–military leader whose legitimacy and power derive from prowess in the field rather than from the mosque. A similar style is that of *sheikh* which obliges followers to rally in protection and fighting readiness.

The profile of Osama bin Laden represents a profile of a terrorist organisation which is unlikely to go away. It will continue even after the death of its founder. For the rest of the world there is the sobering thought that voicing detestation of this Midas figure has raised him as a hero and possibly sanctified him as a blessed martyr in a part of the world where such veneration has a political and destabilising salience.

As American forces set out to invade Iraq in February 2003 (an attack widely thought unnecessary and illegitimate), the White House was asking the question: is there an unholy alliance between Osama bin Laden and President Saddam Hussein? Authoritative opinion fails to see the religious terrorist and the secular dictator maintaining any credible relationship. More clearly there are signs both of distress and vigorous antipathy towards the United States, in particular in the *ummah*, the body of Muslim believers around the world. Osama bin Laden, from an unknown vantage point, continues to berate America. He chooses his words most carefully, to condemn 'the crusaders' who 'storm in like locusts' with attacks on Islam's strongholds in Afghanistan and Iraq. There are also stern warnings to Israel over their intolerant treatment of the Palestinians. Muslim newspapers, websites and politicians echo this. Terrorist attacks are surely in the offing, for as Hosni Mubarak, President of Egypt, has declared, the American action in Iraq 'will create one hundred bin Ladens'.

These three profiles illustrate men whose threats to society originated and developed as deliberate acts of principle rather than on account of unrestrained impulse. Each of the three terrorists can be thought of as being physically responsible for their violent behaviour, which they justify, yet they appear morally detached at the same time. They are in a state of 'moral disengagement', as the eminent social psychologist, Albert Bandura, puts it. Is this a state and a mechanism markedly that of the terrorist? This is a point to be returned to in Chapter 8, which discusses a number of ethical issues.

6   Tactics and methods

Accounts of terrorists and terrorism sometimes leave the reader in doubt as to the distinction between strategy and tactics. Soldiers down the ages have been taught that a *strategy* is the planning of a campaign taking into account a comprehensive reckoning of one's own goals and resources and with a shrewd estimate of the enemy's objectives, intentions, likely moves and resources. It is in a sense a detached consideration. *Tactics* are the feasible steps to take in order to meet the goals outlined in the strategy. Tactics size up possibilities and limitations: they will determine the methods that are most practicable. Those deciding their tactics and methods are not detached – they are very much engaged in handling a situation and they may have to 'play it by ear', modify, even retreat. As an example, the IRA has had a fairly consistent strategy over the years of freeing Ireland from London's 'suzerainty'. Liberation strategies the world over have sought to attain long-term independence. Tactics and methods have been devised as appropriate.

Terrorist methods: some examples

Tactics require agreement and decision as to methods. These are some of the methods terrorists commonly employ:

> arson; bombs in vehicles; remote controlled explosions; 'Molotov cocktails'; biological and chemical materials disseminated offensively; grenades; gun attacks (hand and automatic); mortar attacks; attacks with rocket launchers; knife attacks; machete attacks; hijacking of vehicles and aircraft; hostage-

taking; kidnapping; torture; sabotage attacks on buildings, public facilities and transport; assassination (of individuals and groups); letter bombs; stoning; vandalism leading to serious injury or death.

These are some of the common targets:

aircrafts; airports; banks; commercial premises; hotels; government officials and their offices; discotheques and theatres; diplomats; military bases and personnel; buses; railways; roads; shopping areas; subways; markets; religious and political figureheads.

A common feature of contemporary terrorism is that, despite lessened frequency over recent years, the number of people killed and injured has grown. This is partly on account of techno-terrorism: the use of remote-controlled and delayed-action devices and more sophisticated means of communication. Detection and prediction of many modern methods are becoming more difficult. Prediction is often almost impossible where the terrorist has primed a car bomb, carries an explosive device around the waist, or has an intended target in his rifle sights.

Trailblazers and tactics: a historical note

The wide array of methods used by terrorists yesterday and today owes something to the significant influence of several writers – trailblazers in terrorism. A historic debt to them has been freely admitted. These trailblazers have included Andreas Baader and Ulrike Meinhof (with their associates) in Germany, Abraham Guillén and Che Guevara in Latin America, Fidel Castro in Cuba and Frantz Fanon in France. In all cases, the highpoint of their activity was in the 1960s but it is evident that their influence has been long-lasting.

An important point to make here is that apart from the two Germans these writers were guerrilla theorists to begin with, that is to say, in line with a previous definition in this book, they were matching themselves against institutional forces such as military personnel and facilities. They saw themselves as being in the vanguard of those who would fight for freedom. Violence would be inescapable but they were not making a brief for the indiscriminate violence of the terrorist. Baader and Meinhof, on the other hand, were certainly able to incorporate indiscriminate violence even if their message did not get across to a wider German audience. They were fighting for freedom in several respects. Aggressively, they were warring against those forces of repression and power they saw epitomised by the German state, or by United States influences or by the Cold War barricades of NATO. Defensively, they set out to protect fellow students and trade unionists against discrimination. There was a following for a time for ideas such as these in the volatile Germany and Italy of the 1960s, even though their intellectual crudity and political naïveté increasingly lost them more and more adherents. Their notion of using violence at all costs and calling for collaboration with the Vietnamese and with the Palestinians did not have much of a response among the more thoughtful activists in Asia or the Middle East. Pragmatically, while not dismissing violent methods they were much more interested in tangible constitutional gains in a step-by-step process. Dreams were not for them.

Abraham Guillén made a significant contribution to guerrilla ideals 20 years after the Second World War (Gillespie 1982: 79–82). A veteran of the Spanish Civil War, he later made his home in Argentina. His experience of fighting Franco's dictatorship in Spain made him above all a persuasive tactician. The guerrilla must operate with three basic principles in mind. First, that even in a democracy, the chain of protest that works through meetings, demonstrations, propaganda and industrial strikes will inevitably engulf everybody in 'total war'. For that one must be ready. Second, the essence of guerrilla success would be to bring in the whole community not as passive lookers-on but as active co-participators. One must not terrorise them. It must be 'all for one and one for all' in an engagement that was not coercion. Third, no military victory in itself would guarantee lasting improvements for a society. Guerrilla efforts had to be 'politically convincing' to the widest of constituencies.

Total warfare required decisive tactics. There is a tinge of Maoist doctrine in Guillén's first step of fanning out in remote country areas before penetrating the town. Small cells of five to six men, lightly armed, rapidly moving, would punch carefully directed blows at a security force taken by surprise. This is 'low-intensity conflict' puzzling the enemy and not hazardous to local people whose sympathies will be clear. In time, the cells will come together as an army of liberation, welcomed by collaborative communities.

Guillén's manual for the guerrilla seems to have been read widely at the time. People as different as Che Guevara, Fidel Castro, Nelson Mandela, Colonel Quaddafi, and the top echelons in Hizbullah and the IRA have all acknowledged a reader's debt. Both Guevara and Castro esteemed Guillén's tactical innovation and directness but, in their writings, showed a degree of reservation. After all, they were seasoned campaigners. They were interested in Guillén's assumption (really a classic calculation used by guerrillas and terrorists) that group violence will lead to harsh repression, destroying the liberal façade of government and recruiting popular support. Guerrillas are ready to take on repression and the guerrillas will win. Nevertheless, was there not an element here of overestimating guerrilla power and underestimating that of the security forces? A coordinated counter-guerrilla strategy could muster overwhelming resources, using technology and air power. Would it really be easier to mobilise a protest force in thinly populated countryside? If the guerrillas in their desperation became terrorists, lashing out at civilians, the terror would only lead to counter-terror.

Despite the wariness of Ernesto 'Che' Guevara in responding to a theorist such as Guillén, much of what he undertook and led in Latin America followed the direction of the veteran. Guevara, in his book *Guerrilla Warfare* (1969) built a theory of armed struggle which he termed *foquismo*. Central to this was the mystique of the 'heroic guerrilla', a quasi-romantic figure sure to appeal to young Latin Americans ready to risk their lives to follow a new creed. There were three cardinal principles in that creed:

- There is no point in waiting for 'conditions to be right' or for 'participants to be ready'. The revolution is now.
- Prompt action brings immediate success. With popular backing revolution is assured.
- *Foquistas* (guerrillas) are the touchstone of revolution, the initiators, architects of progress.

Guevara, a trained doctor, was confident he knew men's minds and hearts. Tactics to be employed would bind recruits into an enterprise which they shared and in which they felt fulfilled. Violence, where they had recourse to it, could serve to whip up a fighting spirit and consolidate the ranks though, of course, there was the risk that going too far would alienate possible sympathisers. With the guerrilla turned terrorist, in most eyes, violent methods must not be acts of vengeance yet they might be needed to dislodge the 'terror of exploitation', to purge the old, to bring in the new and a progressive society. However violent methods became, they would rock an opposition in months, something that years of diplomacy and compromise could never achieve.

Guevara's methods (which he had perfected alongside Fidel Castro, a fellow partisan in Cuba) reveal the influence of Guillén and Mao Tse-tung. Bases must be set up in the rural outback. Highly mobile small groups, knowing the terrain intimately, would infiltrate larger army and police detachments. Guerrillas must be self-sufficient, relying on local people providing food, shelter and information. Moving into towns would not be possible unless methods used were appropriate to deploying in confined spaces, to operating where visibility might be dangerously reduced, and in streets where an enemy could use vehicles – all this would transform the *foquistas* into 'urban guerrillas'. Certainly, in the crowded towns, there was the possibility of civilian damage and casualties. This was a small price to pay considering the 'selective terrorism' of an autocratic regime bleeding the people. In any case, the enemy security force would now term the guerrillas 'terrorists'.

Guevara's maxims were widely taken up in Latin and Central America, by those fighting anti-colonial wars in Africa and south east Asia and, to some extent, by the African National Congress in apartheid South Africa, not always enthusiastically. Leaders, though, who had campaigned hard and long must have found Guevara's assumption of fighters being ready at an instant rather incredible. Liberation campaigns usually took a long time to prepare. Rarely were gains achieved by some quick-fire unanimity of intent. Rather, for Mao there was a 'long march' to organise and tread and for Mandela a 'long walk to freedom' (after the leader's 37 years in jail).

A final trailblazer, a 'methods man', was Frantz Fanon, a West Indian educated in France. His book *The Wretched of the Earth* was published in 1968, a year when there was much terrorist turmoil in Europe and Africa. It seems to have been well thumbed by liberation leaders conducting battles against imperial rule. Fanon acknowledged that the process of breaking free from colonial shackles would be hard and rough and bloody. Dignity, self-respect and life itself could not be satisfied under dominance. In similar terms to Guillén and Guevara he spoke of covert, unorganised resistance to oppression flaring into overt, organised warfare. Methods to free those in slavery would be 'no holds barred' with violence a legitimate instrument. The terrorised 'wretched' might have to terrorise in return. Fanon's readiness to admit terror methods to the liberationist arsenal almost certainly influenced the tactics and the methods of sabotage, shooting, arson and murder adopted by General George Grivas fighting the British in Cyprus, the Communist irredentism in Dutch Indonesia, and some of the atrocities that poisoned fratricidal feuding in Central America and even in Northern Ireland.

Terrorist methods in debate: yesterday and today

The tactical suggestions of the trailblazers were not altogether acceptable to freedom fighters. In fact, they presented a dilemma, particularly to Mandela and to certain groups in the Middle East. Do we use terror methods, or do we not? When are violent methods so unproductive that tactics must be less violent?

South Africa's debate

The debate that was ongoing in apartheid South Africa is a most interesting one to recall (Mandela 1997: 132 ff. and Whittaker 2003: 239–44). Nelson Mandela, in his autobiography *Long Walk to Freedom* (1997), describes the 'soft' methods of the 1940s and 1950s – civil disobedience, non-cooperation, boycotts, strikes, individual and mass defiance. Afrikaaner governments met these with a State of Emergency which would feature press censorship, forced eviction and confinement in special areas. The African National Congress (ANC) gradually concluded that such methods, however well-planned and executed, could only result in relentless security crackdowns. Bullets replaced tear gas and water cannon in 1960 and in that year police brutality at Sharpeville gunned down 69 unarmed protesters. No black solidarity movement could make headway against white rifles and law. Were 'hard' methods, 'violent' methods, now the only way? White power spoke of a 'total onslaught' strategy and repressive 'control' tactics. Black ANC leaders (possibly with Guillén in mind) saw a 'total' strategy as one of armed rebellion. There was much unhappiness in the ranks over this strategic shift, according to Mandela. Was it not best to pursue the inescapable conflict in ways that saved lives rather than threw them away? Tactics that preferred to use violence would surely expose innocent people to massacre by the white enemy. If we went down that hard road, what kind of arms would be needed? Guns, bombs, high explosive and trained handlers to use them?

Looking back on this momentous shift from non-violence to all-out fighting tactics, Mandela traces a reluctant acknowledgement that the ANC would now need to be terrorists. They would now follow the 'path of guided violence'. There was no alternative to their 'progress through battle'. Mandela, no soldier, must now recruit a military wing for the ANC, to be known as 'the Spear of the Nation'. He spent hours, he says, examining the tactical writings of Fidel Castro, Che Guevara and Mao Tse-tung. He studied closely accounts of guerrillas in Kenya, Algeria, Israel and Ethiopia.

Four types of terrorist tactics were considered by the ANC higher command: sabotage, guerrilla warfare, terrorism, open rebellion. The debate seems to have been an anguished one. Would not terror methods, the bomb and the shootings, alienate the wider public and, like rebellion, invite savage government reprisals? Guerrilla operations meant steady training of volunteers, entirely familiar with the bush but then up against the government's mobile 'control squads' and gunships. Sabotage seemed the best of methods. For the least manpower there could be forays against selective military installations, power plants, factories and railways. 'Soft' terrorism on these lines ought to erode government complacency and even move them towards negotiation. If sabotage did not produce results, then, as Castro and Guevara would advise, they moved into guerrilla warfare.

Predictably, the apartheid regime condemned liberationist tactics as irresponsible terrorism. There was, indeed, much brutality and sheer terrorising of black people by the young, extreme flank of the ANC who engaged, too, in a bitter struggle with rival groups. Even so, whatever the success of the new tactics in military terms, there were considerable political dividends. As in Northern Ireland, when the IRA had secret talks with London, so in South Africa terrorist and government ministers talked in private in the late 1980s. Ten years of plodding negotiations finally brought the collapse of apartheid soon after 1990. Black and white were now to share government in a Rainbow Nation. After 37 years in jail, Nelson Mandela, arch-terrorist (retired) became South Africa's first black President.

Mandela does not mention in his autobiography a wider debate about terrorist methods, namely, in the United Nations. Member states of the UN were faced with the issue of endorsing the legitimacy of armed struggle to resolve internal conflicts. Were terrorist operations to be approved? Lawyers, consulted by the UN, ruled that it is permissible to use violence only in extreme situations as a final response to systematic violation of human rights. Violent methods to resist violation should be 'proportionate to the gravity of that situation'. The bomb would not do. South Africa's blacks did not take kindly to such findings. Their tactics were throttling the life out of apartheid by the late 1980s. Granted, their resistance methods unavoidably took lives but could the international community sit on its hands and take refuge in non-violent methods while a persecuted people exploded? The UN's General Assembly had already, in 1976, challenged South Africa in establishing 'the inalienable right' of those suffering under apartheid to use all available means of opposition including 'armed struggle'. Terrorism was not being blessed but 130 nations and 400 liberal non-governmental organisations (NGOs) were explicitly supporting a liberation campaign. Freedom fighters might well use terror methods in desperation.

Methods debate in the Middle East

Lebanon's debate

Controversy about terrorist methods has been rather more complicated in the Middle East compared with South Africa (Saad-Ghorayeb 2002: 145–7, 160). Lebanese and Palestinians have bitterly taken sides over the question of using all-out methods. Do the car-bomb and suicide killings contravene the teachings of the Koran? Are we squaring the circle if the reply, in justification, is that violence can be defensive against extreme provocation and ill-treatment?

Lebanon's violence has increased on two fronts, internal and external. Within Lebanon, over 40 years, a Shi'ite community has mounted revolutionary insurrection as a protest against Christian domination. When this protest was accompanied by virulent anti-foreign propaganda, a whole new arsenal of terror methods was introduced by a militant wing, the Hizbullah, formed in June 1982 against the United States and Israel, seen as their chief enemies. Muslim clergy, secular politicians and a fiery press were all able to find room for violence as a means to a defined end. Political assassination, aircraft hijacking, suicide bombing, attacks on Israeli settlements, were all methods to be used.

The last 10 years have seen increasing concern in government and intellectual circles in Beirut. Islamic doctrine is committed to respect for life and cannot find a place for suicide tactics. If terrorists embark upon a *jihad*, an obligatory mission, then Israel and the West will see this as completely uncompromising and there will be no negotiation and reconciliation. There is a clear gulf in thinking between the older, better educated and travelled 'realists' and younger 'idealists' waging a redeeming, unending struggle.

The Palestinian debate

A similar divide over methods is to be found among Palestinians. The world has seen on TV screens each week since 1987 the *intifada* demonstrations of unemployed youth. Bullets, or car bombs, suicide fanatics bring a terrible counter-response. The Palestinian leader, Yassir Arafat, himself condemned as a terrorist, tries to lessen a vicious confrontation but has to deal with Palestinian groups at odds over methods. A liberal wing, the Tanzim, stand by democratic, peaceful methods, rejecting the notion that violence might persuade beleaguered Israelis to talk. More fundamental Muslims, the Hamas, insist that only their destructive repertoire of methods can free Arab territories. The Islamic Jihad hold only to the elimination of Israel, without any consideration of the costs likely to be involved. A fourth group are aged 18 to 22, desperate in downtown shacks or refugee camps. They will never disband. They will never compromise. They are to blast and burn Israelis.

Israel's selective targeting of Palestinian terrorists has removed a middle layer of leadership who might have restrained angry youth and even been prepared to seek a truce. These men were joined by some spiritual leaders, influential journalists and writers, and by diplomats posted abroad. Stop the terror – rather speak and listen – is their message. They are well aware of the heavy insistence of the United States and of Israel in May 2003 that Palestinian terrorism must absolutely stop within two years if Stage One of a 'road map' for Middle Eastern settlement is to be implemented.

Libya's debate

The main issue discussed above is the extent to which any group or state can go on to adopt terrorist tactics. Which ideals and policies energise political violence? These questions have been explored by Libya's leader, Colonel Muammar al-Quaddafi. Described by the *New York Times* as a 'warring, whirling dervish', and a master of capricious, vicious foreign policies since his accession in September 1969, Quaddafi has been described by others as a studious reader, a careful listener and a pragmatist who, with an ideological 'think tank', aims to convert theory into reform practice. His thinking was clearly behind the publication in 1975 of a so-called *Green Book* (Whittaker 2003: 74–8). Some observers regard this book as a terrorists' manual. The statements read as rather quixotic but the fundamental premises seem clear. In the dialectics of revolutionary struggle, we are told, there are stages in which it would be 'wrong' to do without violence. If violence is deemed necessary for revolutionaries it must be 'an organised violence, popular and overwhelming: it will be conducted by the people and for the people'. Following this line of thought is the clear intimation that violence is an exportable commodity, in the interests of international revolutionary socialism. The 'enemy's' ground is to be the chosen area of operation.

Libya has translated principles into vigorous practice. Regarded as the lynchpin of state-supported terrorism, Libya, for 25 years, has been aiding terrorists from many countries with placements in training camps, ample funds and a ready supply of sophisticated weaponry. Again in the *New York Times*, there have been references to Libya as the 'Graduate School of Terrorism'.

On the other hand, the terrorists have come out of the cold. A major deterrent to terrorism export was the punitive air strike on Libya authorised by President Ronald Reagan in April 1986, as a counter-blow to the bombing of a United States army facility in West Berlin. United Nations sanctions followed. Five years of lessened Libyan involvement in terrorist training and sanctuary brought former terrorists into the market-place as Libya revived trading and diplomatic links with the West. In September 1999, Colonel Quaddafi, emeritus terrorist, introduced himself to 20 presidents meeting in Tripoli impressively as 'the leader of peace and development in Africa and other countries'. Terrorism appears to breed self-confidence.

Our understanding of suicide bombers

No discussion of methods can ignore the fact that over the past two decades suicide terrorism has grown into a global phenomenon. It gets 'prime time' coverage on TV. One estimate is that some 15 terrorist groups in a dozen different countries have used suicide methods against their enemy. The impulse behind suicidal methods seems to relate to certain readily identifiable motivations:

- terrorists who cause their own death along with the chosen target and (usually) bystanders;
- terrorists who undertake high-risk missions planned long in advance and readily accept the lethal consequences of their actions (an example would be the 9/11 attack in the United States).

A terrorist group, such as an Islamic religious one, allowing and encouraging a member to give his/her life, will generally regard that person as a hero, promised a beyond-life reward. There is much speculation and research into suicidal terrorism and fanaticism. Social psychologists and psychiatrists, particularly, warn us that the term 'fanatic' should be used with caution. The word is usually ascribed to an individual who displays excessive enthusiasm to attain defined goals, which may be political, social or religious. Dedicated to duty, such a person is absolutely committed and sure about the rightness of the cause followed by any group they have joined. There is no sense of restraint or readiness to consider alternatives. Whatever the consequences, violent methods will be used. In daily speech, though, 'fanatic' may be used to describe people with a trace of obsession, who are to be found in auction rooms, laboratories, sports clubs and churches. The world might be a poorer place, as G. K. Chesterton remarked, without its eccentrics and fanatics. It is worth noting that few enthusiasts in any field relish being called fanatics. Nor do terrorists, on those rare occasions when they are interviewed, admit to fanaticism.

The phenomenon of suicide terrorism has been the subject of numerous studies. Terrorism is a product of strategic choice (Crenshaw 1995: 9 ff.). Terrorists are carrying out acts of political strategy and suicide is an intentional act. Even the most extreme and unusual groups will follow a logic that enables them to find a reasonable way of pursuing extreme interests in the political arena. For Crenshaw this serves as a healthy antidote to stereotypes presenting terrorists as irrational fanatics ready to give their lives. Otherwise, there may be a dangerous underestimation of the capabilities of extremists. Stereotypes will not help us understand the complexities of terrorist motivation and behaviour.

The American psychiatrist, Jerrold Post (Post, in Reich 1998: 25, 38–40), sees extreme terrorist behaviour as the product of psychological forces which drive them to commit acts of violence. Their special logic in so doing becomes the justification for their violent acts. Their attitudes and rhetoric are absolutist and polarising where 'they', the establishment, the source of evil, must be destroyed by 'us', for we are in the right. Taken to an extreme, the urge to destroy may be followed by an act of self-destruction, that of suicide.

Ariel Merari (Merari in Reich 1995: 192–207) deals, as he puts it, with readiness to kill or die and, in particular, with suicidal terrorism in the Middle East. For Merari there have been significant strategical outcomes, and not necessarily the achievement of religious goals. Shi'ite harrying of Western interests in Lebanon in the 1980s was almost impossible to contain by the conventional tactical doctrine and methods counter-terrorism then observed and used. Merari then looks at the problem of defining suicidal terrorism. Briefly, he points to three problems and likely sources of confusion:

- differentiating those ready to die from those seeking to die;
- differentiating those wanting to die and the apparent suicidists who were 'fooled' into suicide by those who sent them;
- differentiating terrorists who merely killed themselves and those whose suicide was part of an act of killing others.

Merari is ready to state his position in debatable terms. Proneness to suicide, he believes, is a continuum rather than an absolute trait and so it is possible to argue whether those who volunteer for extremely high-risk missions have more than a streak of suicidal tendency. Or, consciously, were they so committed to their cause or so thoroughly persuaded by others that while they wanted to live they were willing to accept a high risk of death? As for 'fooled' suicidists, was it their senders who led them to think they would survive the operation, even as an inescapable lethal end to the mission was planned?

Not everybody would agree completely with Merari's conclusion that terrorist suicide, like any other suicide, is basically an individual act rather than a group one. There have been many instances, throughout history, of groups resorting to group or chain suicide though, in most cases, this would not be interpreted as aggressive terrorist behaviour. However, it cannot be ruled out that cultural factors and a process of indoctrination within a group might be so strong that they boost existing suicidal tendency and channel it into sacrificial methods.

Suicide bombers as persons

The prospect of an individual, enthusiastic, devoted, committed, self-righteous, facing certain death fills most people with incredulity. There is a riddle in the fact that such a terrorist shows neither concern nor remorse towards likely victims, demonstrating only a cold, calculated drive for the ultimate in methods and consequences. A riddle, again, is what drives ordinary people to kill civilians and themselves? How is it that a gentle, deeply religious student can turn himself into a human bomb? Deliberately to strap explosive to one's waist, or to load Semtex into a van to send it as a fireball into a restaurant, calls for remarkable fearlessness and a resolve to seek sacrifice.

In June 2002, the *Guardian* was able to interview the families and friends of 21 terrorists who had used suicide as a weapon. They and others in Gaza and Jordan's West Bank had been responsible for 225 dead and more than 1,880 injured. Those who suffered included babies, teenagers, women and pensioners. They were decimated by the blast in shopping malls, cafés, markets and religious buildings. Thousands watching TV or reading press accounts shared the horror. The atrocities had unleashed a torrent of destruction and brought fierce retaliation from the Israeli Defence Force. In spite of that, young and middle-aged men, some women and even children have queued up to offer themselves for a suicide mission. Mothers and the family have been proud, rejoiced, indeed, at the prospect of one of their own taking on a splendid obligation. The volunteer settles all debts, draws up his will and celebrates his last day. There can be no turning back. Paradise will be the longed-for reward – 'somewhere I always wanted to go'.

Most of the terrorists picked out by the *Guardian* were between 20 and 30 years old. One was a 17 year old bomber. Many of them were students in higher education, on the threshold of a career. There was one girl. As far as one could tell, not one of the 21 was known to have suicidal tendencies before they stepped forward for their mission. This is in line with what researchers have noted, though their evidence on this point is mostly anecdotal. To sacrifice your life in terrorist action can be the resort of someone who has suffered the trauma of a relative's death or that of a close friend at the hands of the 'enemy'. The family may have been evicted or incurred a gross denial of human rights. The basic contempt for Israelis flames into unquenchable anger. The honour of the family and of Muslims must be restored. They know that after the diabolical success of a suicide mission there will be prominent attention to it in Palestinian media (and often in Syria and Iran, close associates with a desperate fellow people). Loudspeaker lorries tour the streets proclaiming the glory of the deed. Posters with a picture of the dead hero are everywhere. A flower-decked coffin will somehow be handled across the heads of a milling, excited crowd.

As we shall see in the next chapter, media 'coverage' of terrorists is not often objective. It is not at all certain that a wave of zealots is there ready to fall into the line of death. Nor is it known how many of the suicide martyrs individually wanted to get killed or whether group pressure was so enormous that there was no way

out. In any case, a high-risk attack met by counter-force will generally result in terrorist deaths. There is agreement, on all sides, that
suicide missions represent high-profile action for the attention of
a very wide audience. What is also widely debated is whether
methods as drastic as this, and the likelihood of its 'copy-cat'
image, bring any measurable benefit to a community desperate
enough to endorse them. Many observers have come to think that
a year or two of action enshrined in a cult of martyrdom cannot
but delay a peace process, as it has done in Israel and Sri Lanka.

In conclusion, certain worrying facts seem clearer than ever
about tactics and methods. In the first place, the activities of terrorists belonging to a network such as al-Qaida will resemble a hydra.
One head cut off will be replaced by another somewhere else.
Secondly, terrorists will increasingly move into techno-terrorism,
as we have noted earlier, communicating by means of the internet,
cellular telephones and other aids, making it almost impossible to
locate them before they strike.

7 Terrorists and the media

Analysts of contemporary terrorism tend to agree with the aphorism that, if you do not understand why terrorists do what they do, then it might be because you are watching it on television. The medium, rather than the message, scores highly on lurid images of confrontation and violence and generally low on explanation and question and answer. Another point made, implying a lack of objectivity in media reporting, is that political activists only become known as terrorists when the media is engaged. Statements such as these read rather simplistically but there is a grain of truth there.

Clearly, terrorism as 'propaganda by deed' has been translated today as terrorism by photographic image and recorded sound. The images will have a highly significant meaning and drawing power for both terrorist and targeted audience. Conventionally, it is thought, terrorists want thousands of people as spectators, not necessarily as dead. (A reservation here is that apocalyptic terrorists appear to prefer mass destruction, as recent incidents have gruesomely demonstrated.) Terrorist tactics aimed at illustration by the media are, at least, fourfold in nature. Above all there must be a manipulation of a situation to make its outline graphically real to the onlooker. (There is no place for 'virtual' terrorism.) Second, a situation must be so exploited during attacks and even in quiet periods that there is a suspended heightening of tension, uncertainty and fear on as wide a public front as possible. People are to be intimidated. It is not so much death as unsettling imagination that will be the crucial weapon. Third, and with a public confused, even paralysed with anxiety, there will be a drive to bring pressure upon onlookers and authorities to give in to terrorist demands or, at least, to move these up the agenda. With intimidation goes suggestion that a cause so strenuously believed in and acted upon must surely call for understanding and some support. Fourth, there is justification. Those who are prepared to give their all should be seen as doing that in an attempt to bring about reforms that a victimised public must really want. These are tactics engineered by desperate men that have been radiated through media sources in Northern Ireland and Israel. Almost every day the viewer and reader feels that they are in the frontline. And for the terrorist that is where they are supposed to be. As the old Fleet Street saying puts it, 'it's the power of the pix'.

The modern terrorist engages in psychological warfare aided immeasurably by sophisticated media. In quasi-military terms, this operation is one of attrition to see when the enemy's resolve will give way and finally will crack. Where carefully there will be a cost–benefit appraisal of the opposition's strengths and weaknesses and where and when to attack. The terrorist is the calculating observer, the tactician, the planner. Modern media attention when something happens will yield free publicity as a dose of oxygen. Those targeted in an incident will have that wider audience who will amplify, unconsciously, the impact of the attack. As we have remarked earlier, the terrorised are likely to help the terrorist gain maximum publicity.

The media and the message

Is the journalist the terrorist's best friend on account of preparedness to give terrorist operations maximum publicity? Hardly so, but both deal in publicity. Violence makes the headlines, especially if it happens in a country strategically important for political or economic reasons. The rest of us would be better off if reports avoided sensationalism. Terrorists in cities and guerrillas in the countryside, so it is said, usually place a different valuation on media involvement. Guerrillas can do without the attention of journalists who may reveal fighter tactics and the bases from which they operate.

Terrorists unable to use normal means of communication must use media images to spread their message if they are not to be isolated from the rest of the community. If what they say is to attract attention, then the means by which they put their message across must be noteworthy. Violence on their part will be noticed by everyone else. The bomb delivers a message powerfully: it also leads to general condemnation and repression by the security forces. The message, however cogently expressed, is likely to be reported (or misreported) in censorious terms, something which the terrorists will not have wanted.

An example of the press being unwillingly forced into a terrorist battleground is that of the student riots in the West Germany of 1967. Student demonstrators were out to ruin a state visit to Berlin by the Shah of Iran. Filming on this occasion showed the Shah's entourage frantically ordering their bodyguard to join German police into viciously beating the young demonstrators. A student was killed. Violence and arson spread throughout the streets. Left-wing newspapers lost no time in giving much space to what they termed inexcusable police conduct. There must be closet-Nazis at police headquarters. Students had a right to protest – they were not hoodlum terrorists. Right-wing press organs, predictably, took a different stance. Certainly, the student riot was terrorist. There must be limits to a constitutional right to protest if it went over the edge into violence.

The press–student confrontation in West Germany was to spill over into 1968, a year of great street battles and the burning of newspaper offices and stores. Student protesters, now so prominent in the media, did at least achieve two benefits in their eyes. The resignation of Berlin's police chief was followed by a public investigation by the Bundestag. Media had been used by so-called terrorists as a tactic to reinforce their angry protest. The German establishment had responded by accusing the more radical press of bias and irresponsibility. More conservative journalists had written harsh criticism of student and press alliance. Altogether, media manipulations and confusion brought about a good deal of public anxiety and fear.

Media cannot help but illustrate in some way the messages of terrorists. Most directly, to those in any sense nearby it will be, 'This is what we can do'. Further afield, it is, 'You might be next. Give us what we want'. Perhaps, less stridently, 'Help us resolve conflict – meet our just demands'. Messages such as these have been beamed at homes in Tel Aviv, Jerusalem, Belfast and Madrid and their effects seem long-lasting. There is evidence to suggest in each of the three countries that a showing in the public domain of 'footage' of toe-to-toe confrontation, barricades and blood-stained bomb victims has, of course, sparked into anger, but ever so gradually led to people enquiring: when will this ever end, what is the way out? Governments, responsible for law and order, have to be stern and condemning in public, yet, again, and by degrees, they see themselves as prepared for exploratory talks – in private. Gerry Adams, in Northern Ireland, has admitted that media exposure of the IRA position and activities rarely advanced their cause, and at times severely set it back. There was consternation throughout Britain in 1998, when, despite a carefully arranged ceasefire, IRA activists bombed the market-place in Omagh and killed 25 bystanders. In the same year, much of Manchester's centre was badly damaged by an IRA car bomb. Press and radio universally condemned what appeared to them as the most dire treachery. Yet, despite the drip-feed of images, informed report and comment pushed London and Dublin towards the conference table and a Peace Agreement.

As would be expected, reactions to what one sees and hears are complex, varied and personal. Depiction of a major atrocity is likely to make people share responses collectively. Tokyo, in March 1995, saw a groundswell of loud resentment at city authorities who, it was said, had not done enough to forestall a half-expected attack on underground railway commuters. A group from the fanatical cult, Aum Shinrikyo, poured nerve gas down ventilation ducts. This cost 12 lives and injured 5,000. Anxiety is quickly felt in a sense of lessened security either as an individual at home or when out in the community. The raw edges of assured safety are now grimly revealed. Horror, disbelief, may be momentary, even transient, emotions. More lasting and visible are the changes in daily life that may be imposed. Feelings such as these have been everyday preoccupations of those living through crisis in lands rent by conflict. Resentment, a desire for retaliation, will be a common attitude to the awfulness that the photograph and the printed page record.

Fear, naked and real, will be an inevitable consequence of unforeseen violence. To cause it will be a leading principle of terrorist tactics. It will be fear expanded so deliberately that it acts as a restraint upon freedom and common sense. Most people exhibit a double fear sensation, one irrational, the other more rational. Irrational fears are raised by actual incidents, broadcast threats, false alarms and rumours. They bear little relation to probability. Although the chance of death through terrorism is remote, and that through accidents or serious illness more probable, the magnification in the media of the results of an incident leads to irrational fear, even panic. 'What happened there may happen to me.' Although in-flight bombing and hijacking does not happen very often (the major incidents were in 1968, 1970, 1976, 1985, 1988 and 2001), and in relation to the millions of passengers and miles flown the chances of personal involvement are infinitesimal, there is a reported widespread fear of air journeys and, statistically, a pronounced reduction in air traveller numbers. Pictures of crashed aircraft are, naturally, deeply disturbing. Perceptions are easily distorted; reason soon disconnected. Only the terrorists will come through this calmly. Rational fear is the least disabling response. There will be anxiety but a realisation that the odds are overwhelmingly protective if balance is maintained. Media coverage stresses the dangers and it also reassures. Not 'giving in to the terrorist' involves a chilling set of calculations with a firm resolve to live as normally, and as prudently, as possible. Many will naturally point out that for those living in hotbeds of conflict this is easier said than done. However, reducing fear in oneself is a move against the terrorist.

Terrorism as theatre

There is a strong theatrical element in most terrorism (Hoffman 1999: 132 ff.). As with that most visual and popular of art forms, so in the theatre of violence, actors play roles, and they manage scenes with their victims. The action is carefully staged in time and place, and the highpoint of drama will be reached when players engage with a fascinated audience. Film and television are ideal broadcasters of image and message, either directly or subliminally.

Theatrical impact is facilitated through the pressing crowd of reporters, camera crew and technicians sent to bring an incident on to the screen. Media networks rush competitively to 'scoop' and cover what will then be presented as 'breaking news'. The media industry has its own rules, priorities and expectations as to what is 'interesting' and 'memorable' for an audience. What cannot be ruled out is at least the temptation to make terrorist incidents so presentable in media-conventional terms that objectivity may take second place to the visually gripping. It is sometimes remarked that the intentions of terrorists and of the media are similar. Both do their best to keep the story alive and exciting. Both try to personalise the drama of the incident by describing the terrorist-actors briefly and making more of the emotions of victims and onlookers – their anguish, fear and anger. This is better theatre, short, sharp, even trivial, than dispassionate analysis.

Media responsibility in debate

Representatives of the press and broadcasting have readily joined in public debate about some of the issues raised above. Does 'good television' in the eyes of a network necessitate maximum visual coverage of what has happened? If that is what heightens the publicity, is that not what terrorists want to achieve? Could it be, then, that shots of action may mask a terrorist message from terrorists that calls for reflection? Media and government have collided on a number of occasions, with neither side coming out of the occasion with much credit. Two instances of this are interesting.

It was in September 1972 that eight Black September terrorists affiliated to the Palestine Liberation Organisation attacked the dormitory of Israeli athletes competing in the Munich Olympic Games of that year. Two athletes were killed and nine taken out as hostages. World television was soon on the spot in the Olympic Village. Straight away terrorist demands were broadcast as an offer to return hostages in exchange for 236 Palestinian prisoners. Stage by stage and minute by minute the drama was unfolded. There was a complicated to-ing and fro-ing of German negotiators, and the offer of two helicopters to lift terrorists towards Cairo in the event of a deal taking effect. Cameras and commentators followed every shift in German desperation and terrorist determination. There were interviews with spectators and long-range visual focus on the terrorists themselves. The end came with a bizarre gun battle, the destruction of one helicopter, and the deaths of 11 athletes, five terrorists and a German policeman. Nothing had gone right and there were many who blamed the media for its intense and unhelpful intrusion. For the terrorists it was a grand publicity coup with famous people in a famous location. Some

900 million viewers, so it was estimated, had tuned into terrorism. Germany had been unable to resolve the crisis and had had no privacy in which to negotiate. On the other hand, there were one or two benefits of the disaster. The Palestinian cause looked badly damaged in the wake of the carnage. Israel and Germany were angry with media networks but decided to collaborate in setting up special anti-terrorist units which would handle any similar incident much more carefully.

Media networks were called to account again, some years later, for their eagerness to make a story at the expense of a lower and more productive profile. It was to do with the filming and reporting of a hostage crisis like that of three Hizbullah gunmen hijacking TWA flight 847 en route from Rome to Cairo in June 1985. Extensive media presentation had enabled the world to watch the aircraft being switched first to Beirut, then to Algiers, and then back to Beirut. At each stop a group of non-American passengers was allowed out of the doorway of the aircraft. Beirut appeared in the final scene as American men were whisked away by terrorist sympathisers to hideouts in the city. There they were to stay for 17 days, as the audience held its breath. The dénouement was a United States agreement to meet terrorist demands and Israel (in collusion) deciding to release 756 Palestinian prisoners. This was an instance of television and radio creating wonderful drama for a global audience. The Hizbullah terrorists played, and retained, star roles. They were jubilant at getting excellent publicity at little cost. What the media did, doubtless inadvertently, was to show President Reagan as helpless and 'soft'. The White House was insistent that intense media coverage obstructed their attempts to secure hostage release. The incident, they declared, was manipulated unhelpfully. As for Israel, their policies in regard to Palestinian abduction and jailing – the essence of terrorist protest – stood for all to see on thousands of small screens and news-sheets.

Media presentation – getting the balance right

If there is uncertainty in some quarters as to whether intensive media coverage hinders or helps the resolution of a crisis it has to be acknowledged that network chiefs seem well aware of the dilemma they may face when 'copy' is fresh and exciting and there is a public ready to respond to a bright presentation. How much explanation can they afford to include in an event-loaded depiction? More than one television editor has pointed out, perhaps rather shortly, that they are not a public library. The question, though, remains: does the attention of the media affect terrorist outcomes in unwanted ways? Does over-dramatisation help the viewer or reader get the balance right? A case in point is the day by day reporting on Middle East violence. Journalists themselves have devoted more than one seminar to these issues and the *Guardian* in April 2003 noted some of their agreement. Particularly in broadcasting, where the commentators on the spot have their report time severely rationed, there is recourse to short references against a visual backdrop. Rarely is there mention of the context within which terrorism happens (a point, we have noticed before, so crucial to Martha Crenshaw). A contextual outline would at least briefly remind the public that Palestinian terrorists are operating with several key events always in mind – the Israeli 'occupation' of their traditional lands since 1967, the thousands of Arabs evicted as refugees since 1948, the denial of good soil and water supplies, the rash of Israeli fortress-like settlements. There is a great deal of difference in the way Arabs, Jews and outsiders see the contest and the fighting. Even the vocabulary of a commentator could be watched for bias. 'Savage, cold-blooded killing' could be putting an emotive colouring on an incident. Serious, objective films are frequently said to be too costly to produce. Audience ratings will be too small. Nevertheless, in general news presentation, with editors showing a little more time and imagination in the newsroom, balance might be improved.

The *Guardian* seminar also discussed the presentation of the bombing that devastated part of the island of Bali in October 2002. The image coming across by way of report was of a grievous atrocity committed by irresponsible vandals. This holiday paradise would never be the same again. Something that was seldom mentioned as a contributory cause of the incident was that for the best part of a year the Papuan government had been aware of terrorists training hard to mount some sort of violent protest. They were Islamic fundamentalists lashing out against a secular and heretical government. They had links with the al-Qaida network. Some acknowledgement of these circumstances would have been helpful in getting a full picture.

One aspect of the media presentation of terrorism is the extent to which it can be used by the authorities responsible for security, firstly, to allay fear and prevent panic, and secondly, to reinforce and consolidate a commonsense response. This approach might be termed management rather than manipulation. An instance of this is the way in which the United States set about recovering from the Twin Towers horror of September 2001. The events of 9/11 as pictured were unforgettable. Some of the most amazing filming was done from an interspatial station in orbit over Manhattan. Earth and space were connected in witness. The United States administration had to meet horror and feeling of threat with reassurance. 'Never again' would the vibrant, commercial heart of America and its military nerve centre, the Pentagon, have to withstand attack. Thus, it was vital to present visual images of federal government and the state authorities as thin-lipped and determined in all sorts of ways to meet any future emergency. It was necessary to play down the uncomfortable fact of America's extreme vulnerability by projecting pictures of the Unites States armed might. This, in some way, might restore confidence in counter-terrorism, bearing in mind that America's defences, always proudly maintained, had been abruptly breached not by remotely-controlled missiles but by 19 young men armed solely with penknives ('boxcutters'). Much was made of the bravery and initiative of passengers in the doomed fourth aircraft, Flight 93 out of Newark, some of whom were to tackle the terrorists flying the aircraft, surely, into the White House. Their impassioned 'Let's roll' was to inspire an America fights back movement, more than one presidential speech and news conference. Every day on television the notion of rolling forward in defiant unison filled TV screens and crowded the streets with emblazoned T-shirts and posters. A carefully designed programme of vivid action pictures and muscular rhetoric put the media into top gear as a survival mechanism. After all, Americans were reminded, if it was possible to survive coming down deliberately from the 86th floor of New York's World Trade Center then the resolute, acting together, should not, as the President put it, 'let fear rule their lives'.

The media, the terrorists and the questions

The debate about the position of the media and the terrorist is never-ending. A final point, perhaps, is to do with the questions that the media either asks its audience or refrains from doing so. The situation still causing most concern and controversy is the sort of hostage crisis that held American citizens in captivity in 1972, 1979 and 1985 and had swarms of media personnel in and around the action. Nobody, of course, could have ignored a crisis of that nature and people in most countries were hungry for every item of news. It was the questions, reportedly, that did not help the hostages and may have been of more use to their terrorist captors. Relatives of the hostages were intensively quizzed. What were their feelings towards the terrorists? How should the United States effect a release of the hostages? How would families view the use of force to resolve the crisis? Should the White House use some form of inducement or attempt to strike a bargain? The most irritated by questions such as these were the United States Presidents and their staffs. Presidents Jimmy Carter and Ronald Reagan had to cope with the major stress of a hostage crisis when round-the-clock surveillance was being maintained in Washington and the complex ifs and buts of the situation had to be thought through – away from the glare of publicity (Hermann, in Reich 1998: 211–29). What never helped was for the President to be asked every day in the White House Press Room what he thought about the situation and what he was going to do about it. If the President sidestepped the journalists and asked for patience, it would seem to point up the impotence of the world's greatest military power. Any hint of presidential indecision, magnified on perhaps millions of TV screens, might hazard the lives of the hostages and fortify the resolution of the terrorists. Both Carter and Reagan felt embarrassed by journalists second-guessing and particularly by the damned-if-I-do-and-damned-if-I-don't image so widely hung around their necks. There was the minor matter, too, of a forthcoming presidential re-election and the image of a candidate who had failed to rescue United States citizens.

There has usually been a rather dismissive attitude, a defensive one, on the part of media representatives whose theatrical role is reckoned to be disputable. Bringing the crisis 'home to the people' in their experience is most effectively done by personalising issues, dilemmas and participants. Nobody will ever thank them for what they have done. There is just the slightest chance, in their view, that the media spotlight will ultimately help a nation to deal with terrorists rationally.

8 Ethical and moral issues

This chapter will take a look at a number of ethical and moral issues that arise when we consider the activities of terrorists. First, the label of 'evil' so common in vilification, demonisation and rhetoric. Does such a term help with understanding? Second, the question that continues to puzzle observers of terrorism – is it possible that when terrorists carry out their nefarious acts they are in some sense disengaged morally? Third, are there rival ethical positions in international relations, for instance, that of the 'moralist' or the 'realist', which have some bearing on the way that terrorism is viewed? Fourth, in our perception of terrorism, are there ambiguities blurring moral issues? Finally, in regard to countering terrorists, which moral issues seem important then?

Are terrorists evil?

There is much debate about this question without too much clarity or conclusion. In the light of the basic definition of terrorism as premeditated and calculated use of violence to achieve desired outcomes through instilling fear and insecurity, there seems nothing surprising in the atrocities that result being condemned as the work of 'evil' men. The bombings of al-Qaida are thought 'horrendous' (emotionally) and 'evil' (categorically). The terror methods of the Resistance during the Second World War were seen as 'good' in the context of attempts to liberate Europe from 'evil' despotism. Guerrillas in Cyprus, Kenya, Angola, Namibia, Cuba and South Africa who used violence on occasion to wrest their land free from oppression have been awarded the accolade of 'freedom fighters' and 'heroes' and their departure from agreed moral norms pardoned in retrospect. Destructive violence seemed inseparable from a militant campaign of liberation and must have violated many conventional moral codes, yet, overall, motives were understood as advancing ethical aims in the cause of freedom. It may help objective appraisal if one takes the line of Immanuel Kant who declared (in 1781) that 'the morality of an act is not to be judged by its consequence but by its motivation'. It is not surprising that a reading of terrorist motivation is significant in the categorising we do. There is an apparent simplicity in this if terrorism is understood to be the deliberate and indiscriminate killing or injury of innocent civilians. These are *intended* consequences and morally distinguishable from deaths which may be foreseen but are *unintended* as in the case of individuals defending themselves against criminal attack. Evil is a common pejorative term to express complete condemnation of the first intention and both motivation and consequence are deplored. Clearly, terms such as 'evil' or 'good' represent valuations against publicly acceptable moral standards.

Public condemnation of 'evil' frequently includes a political judgement. Terrorists, after all, are attempting to transmit a political message. A response to that may be outright rejection, putting it in the blackest of terms. Sometimes, the attribution of 'evil' may politically be sketched in global terms, in modern times, often by American presidents. President Harry S. Truman, in October 1945, spoke of the insidious malevolence of Communists, affirming that there must be 'no compromise with evil'. Ronald Reagan saw the Soviet Union as an 'evil empire'. President George W. Bush (the younger) more recently has included certain states in an 'axis of evil'. In this case, evil is a judgement upon a state which is reputed to harbour and support terrorism as well as to behave in lawless fashion and to show much vocal opposition to the United States. Apart from an understandable censure of terrorism it is not always clear which other failings of these 'rogue states' are seen as moral or political anathema. Not every president has hoped that something positive may emerge from reprehensible conduct. George W. Bush, castigating the axis, believes, he says, 'that out of the evil done to America is going to come some incredible good'.

Terrorists and moral disengagement

Are terrorists loose cannon? What process of internalisation takes place as they plan or carry out an operation? Albert Bandura has described in detail (for instance, in Reich, 1998) what he terms are mechanisms of moral disengagement. His argument begins with the premise that as the individual is socialised so moral standards are adopted to provide both guides for conduct and deterrents for any conduct that does not meet the approval of others. These standards function as internalised controls helping us regulate how we act. Self-sanctions are inhibitory, making us refrain from behaving in ways that would violate the moral codes of conventional behaviour in the society in which we live. Bandura stresses that self-regulating mechanisms do not operate unless they are in active mode. They can be disengaged by reordering (Bandura's 'reconstruing') conduct to serve expedient ends, or by obscuring one's own personal part in destructive activity, by disregarding or misrepresenting the harm that activity has caused, or by blaming and belittling victims and their associates.

Are characteristics such as these symptomatic of terrorist behaviour? There is reason to think so, even though some degree of loosened self-sanction can occur in most individuals, perhaps under stress, inducement, or challenge. With an individual who operates as a terrorist, a number of disengagement practices could be expected. Two points, though, are relevant to this. In the first place, the conclusions of Bandura, and of others, must be taken as hypothetical, since there is little firm evidence about terrorist mindsets given their reluctance to describe them to others. Second, it could be assumed that a terrorist contemplating a particularly vicious undertaking will require powerful psychological mechanisms to disengage from reluctance and pity for a victim. There are grounds, then, for thinking that inhibitions diminish for the terrorist who has certain considerations in mind. The reasons for this may be many:

- Non-violent options appear ineffective so violence becomes morally defensible.
- Violent conduct, normally unethical, is unavoidable and can be self-justified.
- Militant action, the only recourse, becomes a moral imperative, a duty.

- Responsibility for terror can be displaced by blaming authority for tyranny.
- Blame for causing hostages to suffer can be displaced by blaming authority for their reluctance to make concessions to terrorist demands.
- Sheltering behind the group ('when all are responsible nobody is really responsible'). Self-restraint is thus weakened, especially where the chain of command is hierarchical. (The Nuremberg Accords of 1945, however, found that obedience to inhumane orders, even from the highest level, or pleading excuse to group pressure, never relieves an individual subordinate of their responsibility for what they do or join in doing.)
- Killing people may be depersonalised where remote controlled devices or mechanised weapons systems are used. Terrorists may not feel directly, personally implicated, and so consequences are disregarded or distorted.
- Terrorists not uncommonly attempt to minimise or deflect attention from harm they cause by focusing the public's attention on inhumanities practised on their comrades by the state, their enemy. Their own violence is exonerated – 'we were provoked: circumstances forced us to do what we did'.
- Tactics calculated to goad the state into harshly repressive security measures are then sometimes used to present such measures as a perverse policy which is 'wrong' and inhumane.
- Where targets for terrorist attack are corporations and institutions, their destruction is depersonalised and may be easier to envisage and carry out than would be the murder of a particular person. In this case where there is no injury inflicted on a fellow human being, there is less self-reprimand and self-condemnation.
- Where victims or targets are 'dehumanised', that is, divested of essential human qualities such as concerns, feelings and hopes, they can be punished brutally. They are deemed unworthy of any human treatment. (There are indications of this in recent terror operations in Kosovo, Serbia, Burundi and among Iraq's Kurds and Shi'ites.)
- Moral disengagement is probably and deliberately reinforced through a process of training in ruthlessness (often, these days,

using videos which are watched repeatedly). This stresses moral rightness, the imperative of militant action, and it creates a sense of solidarity and group esteem for prowess in terrorism.

Operational tactics such as those outlined above raise many moral issues. Undoubtedly, they are full of paradox and constitute few grounds for socially approved behaviour. To translate some of this thinking into action may raise a number of difficult problems, not only for the terrorist but, correspondingly, for security forces. In countering terrorists, whose notions of right and wrong appear skewed, what are the moral considerations the security forces in a democracy should bear in mind? Bandura has set down a number of points:

- Democracies placing a high value on human life, individual rights and general peaceful outcomes find it difficult to justify the use of force, discriminating actions, threats and punishments.
- There are risks in sacrificing innocent lives in counter-terrorist operations. Nor is it easy to argue that curbing terrorist attacks violently will confer eventual benefit on the whole community.
- Harsh counter-measures may be morally condemned by a public believing that 'violence breeds violence'.
- Restrictions on freedom of assembly, movement, speech, information may have to be imposed. Some people see this as illiberal control which needs vigorous justification even when perceived threats are real and a state of emergency may have to be declared.

Where terrorist activity is long-standing and a serious challenge to authority and daily life, there is a tendency to present the terrorists as savage, mindless and barbaric. Put in that fashion, coercive operations to restore peace, and ethical principles, may then be seen by the public as realistic policies and as acceptable from a moral standpoint. Something on these lines was apparent in media and government accounts of events and incidents in Ulster in the 1970s and 1980s and, more recently, in the Balkans.

Public perceptions of terrorists: moralists and realists

In the contemporary world, governments increasingly face the need to contain terrorism and deal with sporadic incidents. Frequently, it is supposed that measures adopted to counter terrorists reflect the attitudes of *realists* and *moralists*. Realists, it is always said, believe that a nation's self-interest is the only guide to policy. They would argue that self-interest, where pursued carefully, is ethically justifiable. It cannot be right, for example, to let the security of a nation like the United States be menaced by external threat. To do one's best to reduce vulnerability must be an ethical duty, provided it is done effectively. Realists, faced with a challenging political crisis, will be prepared to shunt aside ethical considerations and resort to expediency. There was an instance of this in 2002 when Moscow theatregoers were being held to ransom by Chechen terrorists. The hostages had to be released but Russia was determined to storm in, root out the desperadoes, and also send a message to Chechnya that violent nationalism would not be tolerated. Most Russians were horrified that heavy-handed expediency engulfed the theatre in a gassing not only of terrorists but of 126 hostages. 'Was there not an alternative with more patience and thought?' President Putin was asked.

Moralists, in debate, state that a narrow pursuit of national self-interest at the expense of moral principles generally leads to immoral policies and behaviour. Ethical principles (what is good, bad, fair, just) establish limits beyond which certain types of behaviour become entirely unacceptable. At fullest extent, ethics is to do with judgement of actions performed not only in the contemporary world but also as a world ought to be. Essentially, the moralist is concerned with what is right and just; the realist with what is feasible and appropriate. There will continue to be differences of viewpoint. Terrorists captured by the American sweep into Afghanistan were taken off to Cuba, blindfolded and manacled, to be imprisoned in cages at a camp at Guantánamo Bay. Amnesty International and much liberal opinion worldwide have condemned a violation of human rights. There is no recourse for prisoners to lawyers. The expediency of holding down violent terrorists comes up against the conventional norms of human rights and international law and, so far, expediency rules.

Is there a choice, between realist and moralist approaches, say, in dealing with terrorism? Given that an emergency situation usually results from terrorist activities, there is every reason to believe that countering terrorists will be a consequence not of some dichotomy between rival standpoints but of a compromise of approaches. Hard-headed policies will take due account of two sets of preconditions, military and moral–political. The recent attack on Iraq by the United States and a coalition force serves as an example. Overwhelming might and an absence of effective defence ensured a swift military campaign. The moral and political issues that arose were many and complex. A number of constituencies, government, press, public, in all countries, had to be assured, firstly, that there was an overt threat from terrorists (possibly armed with weapons of mass destruction), and secondly, that the threat would be best met by a military engagement which was necessary and legal. Certainly, there was anxiety and protest in many quarters, that this particular approach to Iraq would violate principles of peace, justice, canons of international law and the United Nations Charter. Another point, actively thrust at United States political chiefs, was that the Iraqi undertaking gave priority to retaliatory punishment going much further than the 'active defense' policies of the Reagan era. Then and now, a massive attack on terrorism seemed disproportionate and, in some respects, of doubtful legality.

Intensity of action quite naturally intensifies controversy. 'For God's sake stop this talk of war' was the impassioned plea of Rowan Williams, Archbishop of Canterbury-elect, in January 2002, questioning the moral rectitude of bombing the Taliban and their associates in Afghanistan. Was there nothing else that could be done to break terrorism than to devastate an infrastructure and morale? Moral credibility is endangered, he declared, when random killing becomes a matter of calculated policy and 'we are at once vulnerable to the charge that there is no moral difference in kind between our military action and the terror it attacks'. A response to terror on this scale was disproportionate. There was a need to set in balance actions which sustain some coherent sort of punishment and moves to secure a future more settled and just for all. Punishment of terrorist crime and a gradual reduction of threat could not be put into terms of decisive and dramatic conquest. Rowan Williams has a concluding thought that calling for 'reconceived' (more moral) aims and 'policing' ought to be acceptable to both realist and moralist, bearing in mind that fragile distinction.

Ambiguities in perception of terrorism

The morality of terrorism occasions a lively debate at present in seminars, conferences and journal articles, especially in the United States. A number of very helpful points are to be found, for instance in a report of a seminar, Terrorism and the Law, held in Los Angeles' Loyola Law School in June 2002 (Seto 2002: 1227–63) and in discussion elsewhere on the 'war on terrorism' (Shaw 2001 and 2002).

In the foreground of debate are the moral positions disputants adopt. Seto has three positions as moral referents – consequential, deontological and 'virtue ethics' (Seto 2002: 1240–3).

The *consequential* position is that a terrorist act is morally right if the consequences are considered desirable. Thus a seemingly immoral act, such as killing an innocent child, may be moral – indeed it may be morally required – if the net effect is held to be good, for example, if the child's death would permit the saving of thousands of other lives. 'Freedom fighters' in the forefront of a liberation campaign have probably been viewed in that light by some observers. The means employed by violence to achieve worthwhile ends were considered, in retrospect, legitimate. In contrast, the *deontological* position has terrorist acts as morally right or wrong in themselves, regardless of consequences. It must be wrong to kill or maim an innocent child no matter how many other lives we might thereby save. Seto's '*virtue ethics*' switches from act to actor where the terrorist should never be the kind of person who would kill an innocent child for whatever reason. Alternatively, one could say, for our part we should not be the kind of person who would allow thousands of people to perish or suffer enduring hardship because we are reluctant to see any 'collateral damage'. These positions beg a host of questions among those who scrutinise the foreign policies of states and who may be incensed about the bombing of Baghdad or the zealous strikes against Palestinians by the Israeli Defence Force.

Is a terrorist giving up everything for a cause he believes in to be regarded as indisputably 'bad' or as altruistic? Whatever our moral positions we must surely be honest. For Seto, the question, 'Is terrorism moral?' includes the mirror question, 'Is our response to terrorism moral?' The answer to the second question is important for Seto because a practical advantage may be lost if we respond in ways deemed 'wrong' by others and because, at least under some moral theories, there is an obligation to behave morally regardless of instrumental costs and benefits. Moreover, politically motivated violence 'suffers from an inherent moral ambiguity' that cannot be resolved without throwing into question our existing moral codes (Seto 2002: 1231–2). Whatever our moral position, and bearing in mind any distinction between 'moralist' and 'realist', it could well be that in describing terrorists as immoral there is an attempt to justify our own response to acts and actors. This is an essential ambiguity for Seto and, in regard to any definition of terrorism, it is an ambiguity which has been pointed out in earlier chapters in this book.

Ambiguity can be characteristic of moral stance; more importantly it can lead to our decisions about countering terrorists becoming problematic, perhaps ineffectual. When it comes to choosing a policy to contain terrorism, the need of a definite and prompt response may shift counter-action from moral, judicial means to a much more realistic military engagement. Sending in the army to root out terrorists may be easier logistically than waiting for the courts to meet and act. The easier action becomes the only possible one (Khatchadourian 1998: 115–19; Shaw 2002: 5).

Shaw and many others see military action as a curb to terrorism as 'outmoded', in political terms, and as unethical. When a state authority comes down heavily on a terrorist group there is a disquieting paradox. Can it be 'right' that largely 'accepted violence' is implemented to deal with 'unacceptable violence'? (The question must often have been raised in Belfast and among the Basques.) In circumstances such as these, for Shaw, 'the huge potential for legitimacy in real, concerted acts against terrorism may well be squandered in an adventure with dubious and unclear goals and lead to more innocent victims to lay alongside those buried under the World Trade Center' (Shaw 2001: 8). This must be an issue resonant in those American circles unhappy about United States involvement in Afghanistan and Iraq. There, and in many quarters, the moral imperative must not be seen as ambiguous. The choice has to be for the maximum use of non-violent means because 'political, legal and policing measures are available in abundance to tackle terrorism' (Shaw 2001: 9). Furthermore, preferring the option of counter-violence to deal with terrorists damned as 'mad' or 'evil' closes down avenues towards negotiated settlement, concessions and compromise. Unhelpfully, it reinforces feelings of exclusion, resentment and hostility among those whose tactics are being met with force.

A final point is that moral perceptions reveal an ambiguity that has to do with a power component. Seto, particularly, emphasises this, believing that the term 'terrorism' is most commonly used in political rhetoric to refer to those lacking conventional political, legal or military power. He goes on to say that

> if terrorism is limited to acts of the powerless, condemning terrorism while failing equally to condemn similar acts of the powerful [then it] violates the most fundamental premise of any moral theory that moral principles be neutrally applied. Condemnation of terrorism becomes merely an instrument for the preservation of existing power relationships.
>
> (Seto 2002: 1255)

Countering terrorists: moral and legal issues

The policies and programmes in counter-terrorism will be discussed in detail in Chapter 10. There are, however, a number of ethical and legal issues deserving urgent attention and they will be looked at briefly in this chapter since they follow on points raised above.

Why care about the rights of suspected terrorists, asks the realist, when we all live in fear of the next attack? Terrorists have no moral qualms about their behaviour, especially when it is indiscriminate. Why not crush the forces of terror before they crush us? Does not the protection of civil liberties seem a far-off concern, theoretically desirable, of course, but not to be rated against the real anguish of a bloody terrorist incident? If terrorists fight 'dirty' and 'bend' civilised rules, is there danger in countering them according to finely-drawn, conventional codes?

Controversy over 'dirty' and 'clean' tactics in fighting terrorism was aroused in April 2003 with the publication of a government-ordered Stevens Report on security measures in Northern Ireland. The enquiry chairman reported that, at the height of the 'troubles' in the 1980s and 1990s, a small group of police and the army decided that clearly defined and properly monitored standards of security containment need not apply, so dire was the situation. The use of informers, staged provocation, even of selected homicide, was to draw extremists out of their hiding holes. Neutrality was set aside, so the Report alleged, in collusion between a supposedly impartial army, the Royal Ulster Constabulary (mainly Protestant) and loyalist paramilitary units. Once again, hyper-realists would operate a 'dead or alive' policy in searching for terrorists. This was contravening the rule of law.

Britain has two parliamentary Acts on the statute book to deal with terrorist acts: the Prevention of Terrorism Act of 1999 and the Anti-Terrorism, Crime and Security Act of 2001. In brief, the main provisions of these Acts are as follows:

1999

- The Act defines terrorism as the use or threat of actions designed to further political, ideological or religious aims which create serious risk to public health and safety and endanger life.
- The Act represents a scheme for comprehensive protection of the public to improve earlier and looser legislation.
- The Act will constitute a code under which suspected terrorists may be charged and arrested.
- The Act puts an end to conviction and extradition procedures which were often summary in nature. Each case is to be examined carefully with a right of appeal.
- Any organisation considered to menace public safety and order, for example, by inciting violence, will be banned subject to a right of appeal.

2001

- The Act will be more than ever a comprehensive and rigorous instrument for public protection and deterrence of terrorist activity.

- Certain police powers such as search and arrest, the use of warrants, interrogation and investigation will be regularised and made more effective.
- Any incitement to racial, political or religious hatred will be a penal offence according to published guidelines.
- Suspect financial and property dealings will be frozen and forfeited.
- Suspected terrorists will be certified prior to detention or deportation. There will be a right of appeal.
- Greater security procedures will be put in place to guard government and public buildings, transport links and airports.
- Strictest control will be exercised over the acquisition, transport and exchange of nuclear, biological and chemical materials. Nuclear sites, especially, will be monitored.
- Information about suspected or confirmed terrorist activity must be divulged. Non-disclosure is punishable.
- 'Communications data' via internet, e-mails etc. may be scanned and held.
- Hoaxes on detection will incur drastic penalties.

Ever since 1999, there has been a great deal of controversy and unhappiness about some of the provisions in this legislation. Indeed, in both the British and the United States legislatures, criticisms have been markedly similar. Much of the debate centres on the prime question of who is responsible for definition of terrorism. Is it to be the police, the politicians, or the lawyers? Then there is speculation as to the manner in which such expressions as 'serious violence' and 'serious risk' and 'reasonable grounds for suspicion' could be determined and proved. Would a suspected terrorist be presumed guilty until proved innocent? The burden of proof appears to lie with the defendant. As for the potential incitement to hatred, would this be read as a direct offence, say, spoken at a meeting, or could it be via the written word?

In 1999 and 2001, grave reservations were being spoken and tabled on both sides of the Atlantic, where there seemed to be a violation of human rights. The passage of these legislative instruments was roughly handled, particularly in the House of Lords and in the United States Senate. Were we not overreacting to terrorist threat? In each of these upper houses, the word 'draconian' was used by critics. Anti-terrorist legislation must be the product of empirical fact and not the consequence of hasty judgement, prejudice, assumptions and political expediency. There were moments in both houses when government spokesmen found it hard to stem concern uttered about infringement of a right to a fair trial and immediate access to legal help for those arrested. It was quite 'wrong' (an ethical principle) to intercept confidential internet browsing, e-mails, and possibly to inspect other records and to use the results of this scanning as secret evidence.

The debate on moral and legal issues raised by anti-terrorist legislation continues. This has brought some benefits in that both Britain and the United States have had to pay great attention to the critics and there has been redrafting of the first provisions. There are now extra safeguards. In Britain there is regular parliamentary review in committee and in the United States Senate similar investigating and report arrangements. Both governments have assured the public that the measures they have put into place to deal with terrorist threats are compatible with states' obligations under the Universal Declaration of Human Rights and (in Britain's case) with the European Convention on Human Rights. This assurance is seen as an important backing to the actual machinery for counter-terrorism measures that we shall examine in Chapter 10.

Neither the leadership of fortress Britain nor of fortress America have had it all their own way. While they state in strong terms their realisation that every terrorist attack represents a violation of democratic values, and as such the response must be sufficiently robust to challenge and defeat such attacks, they have come to realise that those values can be debased by hasty and unbalanced counter-measures. To get the balance right, a response to terrorists that is proactive, rather than lamely reactive, demands a keen appreciation of the moral and legal standards that must always apply. Otherwise, the terrorists will triumph.

9   Future forms of terrorism

'Time present and time past', wrote T. S. Eliot in 'Four Quartets', 'are both perhaps present in time future. And time future contained in time past'. That seems particularly true of terrorism. Future styles of terrorism will almost certainly replicate thousands of years of violence for the advancement of certain aims with probably an ominous difference. Contemporary terrorists and those of the future are likely to use what are termed non-conventional or mass destructive weapons. Terrorists show every sign of becoming more sophisticated in, at least, two new directions. They will need more funds to provide hyper-modern devices for they will be, in Simon Schama's phrase, 'capitalists of death'. Moreover, they will be able to operate from afar using remote controlled mechanisms and state-of-the-art communication media. The future is already shaping around us.

This chapter will make a brief survey of a highly technical and controversial field, namely, the forms of future terrorism. The most likely weapons for possible use are chemical, biological, nuclear and cybernetic. In conclusion, there will be an account of the main lines of current counter measures.

Historically, there is nothing new in the malevolence of directing noxious substances at the enemy. For centuries, wells and food supplies were poisoned, and infected corpses and animals left in the path of an adversary. Contemporary terrorists have a whole variety of technical aids to destructive efficiency. Fiction, year by year, accompanies fact. The old terror-world of Jules Verne and H. G. Wells and a host of others was populated by mad chemists, demagogues and fiendish inventors whose exploits and threats to end civilisation at a stroke have fascinated generations of readers.

Modern film, television and video present even more dramatic possibilities, larger than life perhaps on a small screen but pointing the message 'it hasn't happened yet, though it could'. Everyone can now appreciate the possibility, as the United States anthrax letter scare demonstrated, that you can kill 10,000 people for the price of a postage stamp. It will never be too difficult, even for an amateur terrorist, to harness technology devices to disrupt a region's communications, to disable the transport system of a city or to cause the wholesale flight of refugees from terror.

There is no fiction in the fact that chemical and biological weapons are for the taking. The past accrued them when super-powers faced each other during the tensions of the Cold War. The present sees them often stored behind a weak padlock and a climbable fence. A terrorist, before he climbs the fence, can browse the internet and sit in the library and get instant access to very practical means of employing mass destructive weaponry. There is a real prospect, it must be said, that evil and ingenuity will haunt the future more easily than ever before.

Chemical weapons

These weapons are used in two ways:

- In attacks planned to lead to mass devastation. Terrorists, as in the Aum cult's Tokyo gassing of 1995, release poisonous substances in a closed area, or in a crowded urban centre, to cause as many casualties as possible.
- In attacks planned to cause economic damage or result in blackmail. There have been sporadic and, perhaps, fortunately amateurish, attacks on food products, laboratories and pro-cessing plants by such as animal rights groups, anti-abortion league members, far-right groups, in Britain and in the United States.

Chemical weapons have some advantages for the terrorist. The technical knowledge and experience needed to produce these chemicals is much less than that to produce biological weapons. A well-informed chemistry student could do it. For the beginner there is always the information highway and the public library. Most materials and equipment are readily available commercially on the shelf in the form of insecticides, weedkillers and cleaning agents and these can be bought or stolen from shops, warehouses and transporting vehicles. Inexpensive and potent poisons are readily made up from such components as arsenic, strychnine, chlorine and cyanide. Larger supplies can be obtained, either on the black market or, with some ingenuity, from the weapons stocks which many countries have in poorly guarded sites and which have not yet been demilitarised.

Even small amounts of certain chemicals, sprayed or left as contaminants in a confined space, will lead to numerous casualties. There are toxic dusts which are only activated when they make contact with a moist surface such as the lungs. Those that are odourless or colourless will have been impossible to detect before an incident and victims show specific symptoms. Survivors will have to be checked, tested and given follow-on treatment. Terror tactics will yield a huge dividend in panic and general insecurity. Not every terrorist can feel safe, though, handling lethal chemicals. Once the medium of dissemination is agreed there can be problems with the weather, for warm temperatures and humidity will very likely lead to decomposition.

Biological weapons

These differ from chemical weapons in that they are designed for use as mass destructive agents and not for small-scale, specific targeting. They may well be more difficult to deal with since the consequences of a biological attack are frequently delayed. No specific 'event' may be noticeable until infection has spread. This lapse in time makes it very difficult to identify the precise nature of the biological agent and to marshal necessary antidotes and treatment facilities. Ideally, 'early warning' signals to the public depend upon rapid, accurate assessment of a situation. Some symptoms can take up to two months to appear. Many of the substances will be easy to transport and conceal. Biological weapons are hardly likely to be obtainable without access to a laboratory and, once there, skilled knowledge of how to deal with a culture, how to assess its state of readiness and dosage, or how to deal with a packaged supply. Otherwise, terrorists, however scientific they may be, will have to have a contact in a scientific or pharmaceutical establishment. It is doubtful whether many terrorists will be competent enough to produce anything 'home made' given the complex and lethal nature of most bioterrorist materials.

A list of materials that could be used in bioterrorism makes awesome reading. Bubonic plague, typhus, smallpox, botulinus toxin are classic agents known in fact and fiction. Equally dreadful in their effects are the spores of anthrax, the bacilli of smallpox, legionnaires' disease, Ebola, tularaemia brucellosis and cholera. Then there are nerve gases like Sarin, tabun and Zyklon B (used at Auschwitz). Ricin is a substance that came into prominence in January 2003 when small stocks were discovered among Algerian householders in London and Manchester. Security forces arrested the Algerians and rendered the ricin harmless. Earlier finds had been among so-called fascist sympathisers in the United States in 1994 and 1995. Though never used so far on a massive scale, ricin, it is known, is an assassin's tool. One gram, sprayed at a target crowd, could kill 10,000 people. Made from castor beans using low-level equipment, ricin destroys cells and there is, as yet, no vaccine. In Britain there was a good deal of oversight of emergency measures to deal with possible casualties.

With biological materials there are many risks, even for the terrorist (Miller 2001: 51). There is a constant need to keep selected materials under closely-controlled conditions, generally the responsibility of a trained laboratory worker. Few terrorists would have the scientific knowledge to make sure of the optimum quantity for a proposed attack and they would have problems deciding about safe storage and transit when the materials have to be watched carefully for any untoward circumstances which might affect their reliability. It would take a good deal of calculation knowing just how to drop liquid or pellets into the air ducts of a railway station or a town's water reservoir and even more challenging would be to make up the right quantity of defoliant to spray surreptitiously on humans, farm herds or vital food crops from a moving vehicle or a chartered aircraft. Another possibility, though a remote one at present, would be to infect, say, dogs which could then be released in a target area. Disseminating highly toxic bioweapons is obviously extremely hazardous. Anthrax spores can survive for months. Once inhaled, by victim or terrorist, the spores germinate and produce anthrax bacteria that rapidly multiply. Terrorists with a respect for their own lives are going to find high explosives rather safer to handle.

There have been no major outbreaks of biological terrorism so far. Indeed, one estimate (Hoffman 1999: 198) is that out of 8,000 terrorist attacks since 1968 fewer than 60 are to do with attempts to make use of chemical or biological weapons. Threats have certainly been received by governments and rumours and hoaxes abound. Governments are well aware of the risks they run. During the 1950s both Britain and the United States carried out over 200 secret tests over city areas using non-lethal organisms generally dropped from aircraft and, most often, simulating the effects of an anthrax drop (*Guardian* (G2), 12 October 2001). In the wake of germ warfare simulants, precise measurements and observations were logged, enough to convince both London and Washington that the potential for clandestine biological warfare was considerable. That was in the days of East–West confrontation when the risk of a state employing such a strategy had to be reckoned with. Concern now is with what the contemporary terrorist might be tempted to do as a saboteur who could inflict a potentially devastating attack on a town. There are reports, for instance, that representatives of Osama bin Laden toured former Soviet republics and the former republic of Yugoslavia in 1998 on the lookout, first, for fissile nuclear materials and, when they were not forthcoming, biological materials (*Time Magazine* (Special Report), December 1998). It is known, too, that there is a market for 'weapons-grade' biological substances in Libya, Iran, Syria and Iraq where terrorists can find allies.

The prospect of terrorists using biological or chemical weapons has unnerved Americans since the World Trade Center disaster of 9/11 was so closely followed by an anthrax scare. The man in the street is asking what he should do in the event of a possible attack. The press is still full of advertisements for what are termed 'survival kits', ranging from masks and decontamination suits to an allegedly safe collapsible bunker as a living room bolthole. Six months after the anthrax incident of October 2001, American newspapers were taking up criticisms of government laxity in regard to terrorists gaining access to biological research establishments. The United States army's bio-warfare laboratory at Fort Derrick in Maryland, a possible source of the letter-post anthrax, was reportedly managed with loosely ordered security arrangements. A number of lethal specimens had been lost and unaccounted for. Were they already in unauthorised hands? Much closer control and inspection were important, otherwise there was a very obvious loophole for the terrorist.

The anthrax incident in the United States pointed in a very real way to the possibilities that it could have been a bioterrorist attack (International Policy Institute for Counter-terrorism, December 2001). This was the first real attack although President Clinton had received threats in 1998 and 1999 from groups calling themselves American Patriots and white supremacists. No anthrax was actually used on these occasions. In 2001 the first case of anthrax turned up in Florida among postal workers. Five people were killed by powder-packed envelopes, posted chiefly in Trenton, New Jersey, and despatched nationwide. Thirteen others were sent to hospital after inhaling dry spores from an anthrax strain. Anthrax-laden letters were sent to senators, including the leader of the Senate. Capitol Hill offices were closed down and elaborate decontamination procedures begun in Washington. The government, with the earlier hoaxes in mind, was quick to act. Thousands of people were tested for the disease, which could affect either the skin or the respiratory tract, and given antibiotics. Buildings, workplaces, leisure facilities, post offices, even computer keyboards, were minutely examined.

Suspicious powders in envelopes were found in the mail in many countries that October. France, Morocco, the Lebanon, Japan, Pakistan, Lithuania, Portugal, Hong Kong, Slovakia, Australia, Kenya and Brazil were among the 21 countries affected by near panic. Was this a worldwide campaign of intimidation? Was this a second attempt by al-Qaida to devastate morale although recipient states could not all be considered 'Western'? Governments, in hasty conference, decided that immediate investigations must be done by the police and by microbacteriologists. First conclusions were that the global spread of the suspicious mail seemed such a random exercise that it probably was not the action of any well-known terrorist group. They would have had little to gain. Extensive testing of what was feared to be a bioterrorist mailing, in fact, revealed that most of the white or brown powders were harmless, that is, after the first half dozen authentic anthrax samples posted in the United States. Forensic research took the view that the originators of the mailing were not terrorists desperate in violence so much as a graduate scientist, almost certainly in the United States, and someone desperate with a grudge. There was every chance that the first anthrax letters had been sent by a disgruntled laboratory employee from one of the United States Army's research sites. The fact that the attackers used mail as a medium indicated some of the limitations of anthrax as a weapon. It may be possible to acquire anthrax bacteria but it is quite difficult to ensure that it is of 'weapons-grade' quality. This, of course, would be a prime difficulty for a terrorist.

The most effective defences against the terrorist threat to use mass destructive weapons are stated to be good intelligence, efficient procedures to control the entry of people and materials, and the means to respond effectively to incidents. Practically, there is little any nation might be able to do following a terrorist attack with deadly germs. The case of a Scottish island deliberately infected with anthrax during wartime British Government field trials in 1942 and 1943 convinced the authorities that life would not be possible in such an infected area for at least 40 years. On an international level, health ministers from major United Nations member states do what they can by meeting regularly to combat the threat of bioterrorism. They pool research, information and emergency plans, the joint stockpiling of vaccines and anti-biotics, and the coordination of surveillance systems. This meeting of minds is just a first step in containing biological weaponry. Far more effective than a state putting into being a state of 'high alert' from time to time and then, perhaps, relaxing complacently (or fatalistically) is an ongoing broadening of alliance and a full participation by the developing world. All states are familiar with the risk of passing on to the general public too much information about the range of possible dangers and so spreading alarm. On the other hand, details about government counter-action will be useful to any terrorists. One instance of United States prepared-ness to offset terror is the stockpiling of 300 million doses of smallpox vaccine even though the risk of a smallpox attack is currently rated low. In Britain, towards the end of 2002 the Government had ambitious contingency plans for dealing with a biological or chemical attack. Certain newspapers leaked outlines of the planning which proposed a system of 'health cordons' to be drawn around an infected area (*Northern Echo*, 30 December 2002). Police and the army would be deployed to ensure terrorist strikes did not overspill and, if necessary, they would take up positions at railway stations and key road junctions to prevent people fleeing and spreading the results of attack. Inevitably, there is concern in many quarters that citizens' rights might be gravely compromised in such an emergency yet the case for dealing swiftly with chaos and panic can hardly be denied.

Nuclear terrorism

Nuclear terrorism poses a double danger. A nuclear device might be exploded to cause mass murder and devastation. More likely would be the threatened use of fissionable radioactive materials obtained from a nuclear reactor which would be damaged in an attack employing conventional high explosive. Radioactive matter would be released endangering the population at large, disrupting public services and infrastructure, and leading to extensive environmental pollution. There are, of course, hundreds of nuclear reactors in the developed world, not all of which can be guaranteed inaccessible.

Public awareness of the dangers of nuclear terrorism has grown with the dawning of the post-war nuclear age. There is real concern over the proliferation of nuclear industries in the light of the accidents-cum-inefficiencies that resulted in the meltdowns at Three Mile Island and Chernobyl. While there is not much chance that a 'make your own' approach may be that of an intending terrorist, there are very real possibilities that fissionable materials can be traded in the black markets of eastern Europe. There is a ready movement of nuclear scientists, again, principally from the former disintegrated Soviet Union and its affiliated partners where ex-army stocks are large and controls weakly imposed. A combination of illicitly obtained material and the willingness of a recruited and handsomely rewarded expert can produce a 'dirty bomb' which will contain highly toxic radioactive elements with an explosive charge to detonate it. It is feared that al-Qaida is showing great interest in what the American press has christened 'the poor man's nuke'.

It may be so that terrorist organisations as possessors of nuclear resources are more dangerous than sovereign states long deterred politically from engaging in nuclear warfare. Terrorists, it is conceivable, are likely to have fewer moral scruples. Nevertheless, there are dangers for any would-be user as is the case with chemical and biological weapons. Apart from the risk to the individual carrying out an attack there would be world condemnation and alienation. Publicity is the thing that counts for the terrorist. Is there, then, any chance that terrorists might resort to nuclear weaponry? Some experts consider the threat an exaggerated one, yet one that cannot be dismissed (Laqueur 1999: 70–4).

Cyberterrorism

This future form of terrorism sounds deceptively easy to mount. At first glance, information terrorism appears to be a fairly simple and safe means of causing enormous damage (Laqueur 1999: 74–8). At the throw of a few switches, a saboteur, sitting in relative comfort and with highly technical equipment, can shut down power grids, unravel telephone networks, bring chaos to road and rail transport and air traffic control, and break down the operation of pharmaceutical and food processing plants. A 'logic bomb' can be timed to detonate at a certain hour and there will be irreversible damage to software. Computer viruses, if carefully ordered, will completely shut down an entire computer system. A computer can browse through databanks thought to be confidential. Surveillance systems will be entered, examined, and, if necessary, destroyed. Death and destruction can be brought into being at a distance with nobody hostile there to watch. Manuals are available on the internet teaching the tyro how to intervene and intercept. It all sounds the stuff of science fiction. This is the world of rebellion, excitement and power gained at a reasonable price. It is much easier than robbing a bank or besieging an office block. The remarkable thing is that so far the civilised, sophisticated world has not been thrown into complete disarray by those defined as 'terrorist'. Those familiar with the world of computers will know that every day personal and institutional computers are 'attacked' by viruses, 'worms', 'logic bombs' and the interventions of 'hackers'. A general assumption is that hacking is the part-curious, part-impertinent play about of young people with too much time on their hands. There is, undoubtedly, a mercenary and criminal element and some type of blackmailing. Terrorists, to date, do not seem to be hackers but if they are their detection is virtually impossible.

Containing non-conventional terrorism

A separate account of chemical, biological, nuclear and cybernetic weapons should not blur the fact that there is a general relationship – they are contemporary and future devices which the nations' armouries have provided and perfected and which may be acquired by terrorists intent on mass destruction. The only secure approach to containment is to work to curb proliferation of what are, fundamentally, offensive weapons. This road to a safer world was spelled out to the United Nations General Assembly in November 2001 during a debate on international terrorism. The speaker, Jayantha Dhanapala, Under-Secretary-General for Disarmament, put it in these terms:

> Increasing the number and sophistication of weapons and costly defence systems does not protect us from terrorism. Weapons-based security increases the number of weapons and the danger of diversion. We must make greater progress towards disarmament and non-proliferation. That progress will contribute to a safer and better world – one in which terrorism cannot breed and flourish.
>
> (United Nations, November 2001)

Naturally, each type of weapon has a specific programme of containment. Chemical weapon production, stockpiling and use is banned by the United Nations Chemical Weapons Convention of 1996. A drawback here is that the Convention review procedures have had difficulty in grasping the nettle of 'dual use' materials, those precursors of lethal agents which can also be seen as having a legitimate peaceful purpose. A good deal of lobbying and pressure was needed to get states to agree to an inspection regime which would monitor the industrial production of chemicals which could be used as weapons and then put into being a set of firm enforcement rules. This, though, does not make terrorist control foolproof. Difficulties over containment arose in 1998 when a Republican majority in the United States Congress voted that the United States should not be party to such verification procedures as 'challenge inspections'. There were those on Capitol Hill who believed that these inspections were inadequate assurances. The vote was seized upon by many American liberals as an instance of hypocrisy. United States military laboratories were actively researching projects, for both attack and defence, while at the same time neglecting project security at home and weakening it overseas. What would have happened if it were a determined terrorist who walked out with an anthrax sample and posted it in October 2001? Although the United States relies on deterrence of 'rogue states' through the threat of its awesome force, this was seen as inappropriate to forestall an individual expropriating materials.

A more hopeful sign of progress with chemical weapons containment is the recent setting up by the United Nations of an Organisation for the Prevention of Chemical Weapons (OPCW). Ostensibly to monitor the Chemical Weapons Convention, OPCW will be tracking materials which terrorists might divert from legal to prohibited purposes. Verification procedures are to be tightened up considerably with no more than 12 hours' notice of an inspection visit. The long range goal is for destruction of weapons stocks, meanwhile defence establishments are to be guarded as securely as possible.

Biological weapons were outlawed by the United Nations with a dozen treaties and protocols during the period 1971 to 1974. These prohibitory instruments, such as the Biological Weapons Convention of 1972, are unique in banning a whole class of weapons of mass destruction (WMD). Most of the UN's 190 member states (144 so far) are keen to underwrite measures of deterrence with strict inspection routines, although the United States has only very reluctantly and recently agreed to examination of Defense Department laboratories by United Nations experts. Thirty years later a number of shortcomings are clear. The elaborately detailed Convention of 1972 does not, curiously, provide systematic and totally reliable means of verifying compliance with prohibition rules. Again, as with chemical weapons containment there is the possibility of criminal access. The anthrax scare of 2001 and a number of attempted break-ins to research sites (never made too public) have alerted the UN to the urgency of regular meetings of experts to oversee controls. A further problem of emerging complexity is that of progress in genetic engineering which brings into play a host of factors affecting the nature and development of biological materials. It is just possible that terrorists might have contact with researchers and technicians in this innovative field.

Nuclear weapons, in general terms, are banned by the United Nations Non-proliferation Treaty of 1968 and the Partial Test Ban Treaty of 1963. Both of these treaties are subjected to regular review and there is a whole range of less comprehensive treaties and agreements freeing regions from proliferation. As everybody knows, there are as yet no firm and binding measures to restrict nuclear arming by states. Apart from this, at least 50 countries, nearly one in four UN members, employ nuclear energy and have well over 600 power and research reactors. Fissionable materials are, therefore, widely spread. Clouding this awesome reality are the fears of malfunction, radiation seepage and pollution, of inefficient management and security, and of sabotage. The International Atomic Energy Authority (IAEA) was set up in 1957 in Vienna as an attempt to control atomic energy and to regulate its contribution to peace, health and prosperity in global terms. A second responsibility is to prevent 'seepage' or misapplication of nuclear knowledge into military and unauthorised channels. Preventive control is put into force through safeguards devised and applied to put a stop to illegitimate diversion. The safeguards system is based on audit, report and on-site inspection by IAEA staff. Certainly, the threat of terrorist attacks using nuclear weapons has priority in its ongoing surveillance. An example of this work is to be found in an IAEA report of 2001. Since 1993, it is said, there have been 175 cases of trafficking in nuclear materials and 201 cases involving medical and industrial radioactive sources. However, only 18 of these cases were to do with small quantities of highly enriched uranium or plutonium, that is to say, materials suitable for a bomb. The conclusion of IAEA experts is that this 'illegitimate exchange' is not enough to lead to grave anxiety but it is a cause for concern and calls for rigorous international investigation of illicit transfers (where they have been detected), of suspect financing, and attempts at nuclear smuggling. There are some wide open windows of terrorist opportunity in eastern Europe and in south east Asia.

The future risk-picture

A common American expression, often to deal with the chances of a cataclysmic event, is 'risk-picture'. The likelihood of world war has virtually disappeared with the ending of the Cold War though regional hostilities seem unabated. A different threat to world peace is a future scenario in the shape of terrorist groups in many places attempting to deliver a political message in large dramatic terms. Their singleness of purpose may induce them to use methods which result in mammoth terror. This is unlike the terrorism of the past when specific targets were marked down, operations carefully planned and, usually, death and destruction were not on an epic scale. Mass destruction terrorism or non-conventional terrorism using chemical or biological or nuclear devices is a risk-picture that we all now face. For any terrorist contemplating the use of such horrendous aids to destruction, there is a risk-picture in individual terms which ought to make him hesitate. It is not the intention of this book to spread fear and distress about what the future might bring. If we remain realistic in weighing up the possibilities of various dangers, and calm about it, we are well prepared. Reasonable security will depend upon building public awareness via reliable information and assurance that contingency plans are in place.

10 Countering terrorists

Efforts to counter terrorists bring us up against a number of perplexing questions before operations begin. Does so much stress on control and prevention of political violence cloud a necessary attempt to analyse and understand the causes of terrorism? Should we not go as far as we can working with the old notion that 'prevention is better than cure'? Those who ask such questions nevertheless recognise that for people living in places where everyday life is constantly disrupted there is only one question: how do we put an end to it and get rid of the problem?

The prime need of counter-terrorism is to work out policies and put programmes into operation, to pinpoint the originators of violence, to deter them from further outrages, and to deal as best we can with a traumatised public. This chapter has a twofold emphasis in outlining the principles and programmes of contemporary counter-terrorism. A statement of principles can be expected to have an ethical component and issues in this field have already been discussed in Chapter 8. Principles discussed here should be thought of as pragmatic objectives or, perhaps, as directives for those responsible for programming. Programmes surveyed, that is, plans, coordinated strategies and action, are those currently being developed internationally and institutionally by the United Nations, by the European Union and by Britain and the United States.

Counter-terrorism principles

Candidly, the counter-terrorism scene has been a hotch-potch of principles for many years as individual countries have sought to deal with sporadic incidents or long-term activity. In piecemeal fashion this has been a tidying-up-after-the-damage operation, damping down the flames but scarcely extinguishing the fire. Now that contemporary terrorism appears to be a growth industry spanning much of the world, opinion generally calls for a global response and a coalition of some sort to frame principles and practice.

Which are the major principles around which successful strategies of counter-terrorism can be built? A useful survey of principles was published in the United States in 1998, jointly by the Terrorism Research Center and the Department of Defense. The main lines were these:

- an important goal is to *neutralise* a terrorism organisation by weakening it and rendering potential targets more difficult to attack;
- it is vital to build a consensus among agencies, to negotiate ways forward and to share intelligence;
- neutralising must work within the law and discriminate between terrorist perpetrators and sympathisers (a toothcomb is far more effective than heavy boots);
- patience and perseverance are crucial despite frustrating and ineffectual security operations;
- restraint is paramount otherwise much security work becomes unproductive especially if it results in premature or unduly harsh action;
- intelligence about terrorists must be specific in regard to their strength, their leadership profiles, sources of supply and equipment, logistics, goals and affiliations.

A list of principles could be followed by an outline of the issues that then arise. They are practical issues, not necessarily ethical ones. One of the questions frequently asked is this: how can governments most effectively control terrorism while maintaining democratic freedoms? There is much debate about some of the more perplexing points:

- counter-terrorism handled too severely easily becomes reactive terrorism by those in power;
- defining people as terrorists focuses on the security threat and encourages solidarity in response, though it lessens the chances of compromise and negotiation;

- too robust a counter-terrorist drive blurs distinctions between legitimate and often understandable protest and illegitimate, unacceptable violence;
- lack of restraint and a coercive countering policy moves towards repression at the expense of reform. Is there a set of principles in action that aims to balance coercion and reform?

In many countries among those responsible for security there is not always wholesale agreement over principles of counter-terrorism. The security and stability of their nation, perhaps even its basic existence, is menaced by anti-institutional violence. 'This means war' may be a natural response. They tend to resent being hampered by what should be done and by what should not happen. They cannot tolerate 'the tyranny of the shoulds'. Good police work should 'play it by ear' and accord pragmatism first place. Recent experience of counter-measures in Northern Ireland, and earlier in Germany, Italy and Argentina highlights these consequential issues and the understandable attitudes of those who are expected to move fast and decisively.

Counter-terrorism programmes

The United Nations (UN) approach and programmes

To deal with the global threat of contemporary terrorism, two international institutions, the United Nations and the European Union, are devising and implementing programmes. First, the UN, never just a talking shop, has called for immediate, vigorous and collaborative action. The General Assembly of 189 member states has power to design treaties and conventions; the Security Council of 15 members is the executive arm that mobilises members' resolve and persuades them to ratify treaties and put them into effect as enabling instruments. It is for the 190 sovereign states to put treaties and resolutions into practice within their own borders. The Security Council's Resolution 1373 of 28 September 2001, for example, binds member states to modify their domestic laws to permit more effective surveillance and powers of arrest, to hunt suspected terrorists, and to use the most sophisticated means of accumulating and sharing information. Members must report on what they have achieved within three months. Directed from the UN headquarters in New York much is being done to promote research into the causes of terrorism, to convene workshops in coordinating intelligence exchange, in setting up an advisory service, and in providing a crisis mediation service. Member states are being required to put teeth into counter-terrorism in three particular ways – through treaty observance, through the work of the UN Specialised Agencies, and through a new system to crack down on the financing of international terrorism.

Treaties, mainly in the form of Conventions, oblige member states to take stringent steps to root out terrorism:

- *1963–71*: four Conventions make it an offence to act violently and dangerously in an aircraft or at airports;
- *1973, 1979*: two Conventions call for prevention and punishment of attacks on targeted state officials and state representatives;
- *1979*: a Convention criminalises hostage taking – the seizure, detention and threat to kill;
- *1980, 1991*: two Conventions criminalise unlawful possession, transfer, theft and injurious use of nuclear substances and plastic explosives;
- *1999, 2001–2*: a Convention obliges states to take precautions against bombing and all acts, methods and practices of terrorism and to take effective preventive and legal action.

Agreements such as these are translated into action by the Specialised Agencies of the UN. The International Civil Aviation Organisation (ICAO), the International Maritime Organisation (IMO), and the International Atomic Energy Authority (IAEA) will take appropriate steps through consultation and comprehensive projects, each in its specific field. Urgent measures are in hand to improve the security of air and sea travel. Programmes to safeguard vulnerable nuclear material and to render storage and processing sites inaccessible to unaccredited personnel now have top priority. The World Health Organisation (WHO) is carrying out intensive research into possible methods of chemical and biological terrorism. There is an international linkage of states able to provide intensive treatment and aftercare facilities for mass casualties. The Food and Agriculture Organisation (FAO) has an ongoing investigation into the consequences of chemical attacks on crop areas and foodstuffs.

An interesting adjunct to UN conference was that three weeks after 9/11 the organisation convened its General Assembly as usual but gave over an entire week to discussing terrorism and counter-terrorism. An event of rare precedence was to invite New York's mayor, Rudolf Giuliani, to open proceedings attended by 160 states. Unanimously, members backed stiff legal measures to outlaw terrorism and the Security Council's Resolution 1373 banning all forms of support for terrorists. Member states are compelled to cooperate to eliminate terror wherever it is possible. At that meeting and at most open sessions three strong statements were urged. Ambassadors from developing countries constantly pointed out that there was a difference between those legitimately fighting for freedom against oppression or an occupying power and those who resort to indiscriminate violence. Second, there was the reminder that the world must fight not only terrorism but the poverty and under-development that so often fuel despair and violence. Third, concern was voiced that counter-terrorism must never violate basic human rights. (This last point is something that we shall return to later in this chapter.)

A major operation by the UN to counter terrorists is designed to defeat their financing. In North America there is an appreciable head of steam behind this initiative. Canada's Finance Minister, in December 2001, spoke of terrorism in the twenty-first century as rooted on two fronts, violence against innocent people, and, second, the capacity to finance that violence. As a result, states must certainly respond on both fronts. Canada and others would 'destroy their capacity to wield military might against innocent people, and second, we are going to rip from their grasp the capacity to finance that violence' (*The Record*, 6 December 2001). A more colourful reference to an ambitious all-nations programme to clamp down on terrorist funds was that of the United States Secretary for Defense, Donald Rumsfeld, also in December 2001. 'The uniforms of this conflict will be bankers' pinstripes and programmers' grunge just as assuredly as desert camouflage' (*New York Times*, 21 December 2001).

International efforts to counter terrorist activity can be set against a shift from terrorist groups often sponsored by states to a network of terrorists not affiliated to particular states. A globalised terrorism must be met by a globalised counter-response and this is certainly true of efforts to eradicate illicit funding. The former piecemeal and short-term operations by individual states to curb terrorist financing have to be replaced by longer term strategies and interventionist programmes. Termed 'electronic combat', the most sophisticated arrangements will need to be operated by a coalition of banks, taxation authorities and law enforcement agencies. Investments, asset transfers, stock exchange dealings must be monitored. Suspect funds will be frozen, even seized. There will be a watch on 'listed persons'.

How is all this to be done, under a UN remit, when so many nations operate quite different financial regimes? The shape of a watertight financial watchdog, a many-headed one, seems to be emerging slowly. A coordinated search for hidden assets from Vancouver to Bangkok runs across current free market reliance on bank secrecy, offshore tax havens, and financial corporation confidentiality. In the autumn of 2001, *The Wall Street Journal* reported stormy meetings between bankers in the United States and the Chairman of the Federal Reserve Bank, Alan Greenspan, when it took all his powers of persuasion to reassure aghast bankers that effective counter-terrorism, as in the Foreign Assets Tracking Center, demanded the sternest controls – for the time being.

On a broader front, the all-nation initiative to stem terrorist funding comes up against, for instance, three formidable obstacles. Most of all there is the sheer size and complexity of the 'money trail'. Every day thousands of money transactions representing trillions of currency values flash between clients and countries in seconds. Looking closely at a web of these proportions by way of security operations is virtually an impossible task. Security agencies can only hope to scrutinise a fraction of it. Then there is the problem that in Muslim countries much of the money dealing is conducted by the *hawala* (a Hindi word meaning 'trust'), where funds pass 'on the nod' and without documentation. Third, and again in Muslim countries, such as Iran, Saudi Arabia, Kuwait, there are fund-raising institutions subsidising to a very considerable extent an array of political, social, cultural and educational objectives. Most of these bodies, in Muslim lands and in the West where Muslims have emigrated, are entirely above board and do much good, reputable work for their dependants. There is, however, what has been called 'the greenhouse effect', not a term in meteorology, but a reference to an umbrella function where some organisations act as a front for nefarious, possibly violent, political activity. It is fairly clear that many of those subscribing to organisations or benefiting from them have no idea of any diversion of funds to enterprises of which they would never approve.

The European Union (EU) approach and programmes

Another illustration of the globality of contemporary terrorism is that of the far-reaching counter-terrorism which the EU was hoisting into place within days of the World Trade Center attack. The Union's 15 original members will be 25 by 2004 and expansion will increase even further later on. Member states are working earnestly already on a wide canvas of economic, political and social policies and programmes with fundamental human rights always a major concern. Appropriately, fighting terrorism is being accorded priority. The EU, following closely the resolutions and advice from the UN, is designing a comprehensive scheme for improved civil and individual protection against terrorist attack.

An EU Plan of Action for counter-terrorism covers action in six sectors (European Union 2003). The most important ones are as follows.

Diplomatic sector

- Complete support for the United States call for a global coalition against terrorism and for UN Security Council resolutions;
- European social and defence policies to be reviewed and coordinated;
- agreement with non-EU states (Russia, Switzerland, Norway and Israel) over countering;
- advancing a Middle East peace process to stabilise a critical zone and to implement political, social and economic measures to reduce turning to terrorism.

Economic and financial sector

- Scrutiny of money laundering, suspect speculation, transfer, investment, aiming to end these;

- report of the effect of terrorist attacks on tourism, insurance, transport links;
- export and non-proliferation controls on arms, chemical, biological and nuclear materials capable of terrorist use;
- freeze and seizure of suspect assets;
- police and legal cooperation – in surveillance, arrest, conviction, trial, appeal, extradition;
- joint investigation teams sharing lists of terrorists and, generally, intelligence about them;
- check on procedures for passports, visas, immigration requirements. Control of document forging;
- shared scrutiny of policies for asylum seekers and refugees.

Bioterrorism contingency plans

- Databank of possible non-conventional weapons and treatments needed;
- reinforcement of surveillance, test-detection, early warning systems;
- basic lines of improved public communication before, during and after incidents;
- coordination of stockpiles, antidotes, treatment supplies and equipment;
- pooling of medical, scientific, research, expertise and personnel. Liaison with WHO.

No elaborate programme such as the one above can guarantee that more than a score of states will interpret directives in similar fashion. Bringing legal and home affairs matters into common focus is a relatively new experience for many European ministers. The last two years have seen them almost breathlessly engaged in a series of summits, workshops, conferences and media interviews. Most European states have had no specific laws on terrorism and have dealt with any terrorist attacks under ordinary criminal law. Now, the European Parliament in Brussels and the EU Court in Strasbourg talk of an 'homogeneous judicial area'. Already, three legal innovations have been tabled and ratified. First, there is to be a common definition of terrorism and its offences (murder, kidnapping, financial extortion, cyberterrorism).

Second, a European Arrest Warrant will prevent terrorists from taking advantage of varying European legal systems and this will also simplify and accelerate extradition procedures. Third, a common, graduated penalty scale will operate, providing for sentence-on-conviction of 2 to 20 years. It is only to be expected that a raft of measures such as these raises concern and some protest about apparent diminution of human rights, a matter, as we have said earlier, that can be looked at towards the end of this chapter.

British and United States approaches and programmes

Between these two countries there is much common ground over counter-terrorism, in theory and in practice. It will be convenient to take a brief look at their similar programmes:

- an inventory of the reported aims of specified and suspect organisations is to be on the 'bulletin board' without delay;
- surveillance in so-called vulnerable areas is to be stepped up;
- maximum physical security and checks of personnel, buildings and everyday routines are to be strictly and urgently implemented in scheduled places;
- recruitment and training of special units to prevent terrorist attacks and to 'cover' incidents when they occur;
- use of informers and undercover agents where deemed necessary and practicable;
- monitoring, searching and inspection of computer traffic and documentation subject to legal advice and permission;
- a policy of no-ransom to hostage takers and no concessionary negotiations with terrorists;
- a repertoire of sanctions to be applied to suspects, for instance stop-and-search, charge and arrest, appeals procedure, internment, extradition;
- 'last-chance' opportunities for dialogue and mediation with potential or arrested suspects (more honoured in the breach than in the observance, it seems).

These programmes, in Britain, are being operated by the Home Office, a special department in the Foreign Office, and by an elaborate framework of collaboration with the Services and local authorities.

Generally, in the case of the United States and its attitudes to countering terrorism, a sea-change is recognised. The greatest world power, exceptionally secure, had its vulnerability demonstrated in 2001. Nothing really protected the 49 states from a recurrence unless they did it themselves. No longer would head-in-the-sand isolationism prove a bulwark. A robust alternative was strength at home and interventionism abroad, supported, in the President's words, 'by the collective will of the world'. To lend credibility to this statement the President, within weeks of September 2001, had met leaders from 51 countries to build support for unified efforts. To those countries whose response seemed cold or uncooperative he had a brusque message (perhaps typical of the great fortress of capitalism): 'If you do business with terrorists, if you support them or sponsor them, you will not do business with the United States'. The United States, he said, would provide a global dragnet. 'Terrorists are in the shadows, they try to hide. But terrorism has a face and it will be exposed for the world to see' (*Washington Post*, 15 October 2001).

An Office of Homeland Security (with an initial budget of US$20 billion) would mastermind Federal counter-terrorism. The stages of countering would be identify-prevent-disrupt-defeat terrorism. States would integrate communications and activities with 93 anti-terrorist task forces. Public service announcements would make sure Americans understood what was afoot. To forestall any prospect of chemical or biological terrorism would be the remit of an Office of Public Health Preparedness. What some were christening 'e-terrorism' would be the concern of an Advisory Committee for Cyber-security. To defeat the financing of terrorism is a major concern for Washington as it is for the UN. The United States State Department reported that 142 countries were acting to freeze suspect assets. By January 2002 in the United States some 153 individuals and organisations had had their funds either frozen or confiscated. Investigations were in hand with the Foreign Terrorist Tracking Task Force and the Terrorist Financing Task Force. This was to be a complex shadowing and securing operation. On the ground highly mobile, lightly armed forces stood by in readiness to operate a 'quick reaction alert' if need be. Once again, the White House couched terms in black and white:

Terrorism thrives on the element of surprise and one of the key ways to defeat it is to take the fight to the terrorists, to deal with them at a distance, to hit the enemy hard in his own backyard, not in ours, and at a time of our choosing, not his, acting always in accordance with international law.

(*Herald Tribune*, 25 February 2003)

Counter-terrorist programmes are being exported by Britain and the United States to many Middle Eastern countries and also to republics on the fringe of Russia where state authorities are having to deal with Islamist extremism. Georgia is an example of this, where British and United States army trainers are helping security forces there improve their capabilities.

Both London and Washington intercept what they term 'background noise' from communication exchanges across the world. They listen in to thousands of conversations, especially those emanating from Arab countries. They then have the problem of how to warn the public of possible dangers without provoking panic. A programme termed 'protect and survive' has to reckon with a large amount of complacency in the general public, even when a state of high alert is proclaimed. Nothing can be worse for the counter-terrorists' image than when they are accused of 'crying wolf' when a very public warning of impending attack turns out to be groundless.

Counter-terrorism and human rights

Has the pendulum swung too far to the detriment of human rights? Are counter-terrorist principles and practice being pushed so urgently and pragmatically towards a degree of expedient risk-management that, of course, lives are saved, but the rights of ordinary citizens are down-rated and eroded? Does 'tailored containment' (a White House expression) compromise in some respects civil liberties and put shutters up on an 'open society'? Questions such as these are heard in numerous places. Again, there is a broad resemblance between liberal critics on both sides of the Atlantic.

In the foreground of a large complex of differing viewpoints is the continuing and stark difficulty of defining the terrorism we are supposed to be countering. The eminent international lawyer,

Rosalyn Higgins, considered in 1997 that terrorism had no legal significance. She believed, basically, that terrorism was merely a convenient way of alluding to activities, whether of states or individuals, which were widely disapproved of and where the methods used were unlawful. The term terrorism, for her, is at once a 'shorthand' to refer to a variety of problems with some common elements, and also a method of indicating community condemnation for the conduct concerned. If that is a considered legal position then the ground for counter-terrorists is shifting sand, for the government minister needing to act quickly, for the lawyer circumscribing legitimacy, and for the liberal who holds that human rights are non-negotiable.

Since Britain and the United States have comparable counter-terrorism policies, they have to expect similar criticisms. In the case of Britain, critics can be seen to focus, particularly, on half a dozen issues. First, can it be right that the British Government has put into suspense its obligations under the European Human Rights Convention? Second, it appears that foreigners are being treated with more hostility than Britons. Bringing immigration rules to bear rather then common law curtails a number of rights, certainly the right to seek asylum. In Britain and other European countries, refugees and asylum seekers are increasingly regarded as militant. Suspicion and over-zealous security measures easily exploit divisions between people of different origins and faiths and breed xenophobia. Third, in the case of possible conviction for terrorism a tribunal will circumvent normal trial process. Much will be secretive and the hearing of evidence will be closed rather than open. Fourth, if defendants are held because they are considered to be endangering society then it is they who have to prove their innocence. Fifth, is habeas corpus also suspended? Section 41 of the Terrorism Act 2000 allows a suspect to be held for seven days. Is this not arbitrary detention? Finally, does the Big Brother nature of heightened surveillance and information collecting violate basic rights to privacy quite seriously?

Unease in the United States about counter-terrorist legislation has been marked. The American Civil Liberties Union, for instance, made its dissatisfaction over the hastily-passed USA Patriot Act of 2001 very clear. Much that the Federal authorities could do appeared to have only the slightest legal sanction. Suspects could be rounded up and detained without access to legal aid. Properties and people occupying them were liable to be searched without notification. 'Institutional snooping' was the worst where 'roving wiretaps' interfered with privacy and confidentiality. There would be few limits to counter-terrorism if it were pursued with rigour. Would the FBI tap all computers in a library if a suspect was thought to be using just one of them? If the direction of much of the surveillance was, as it was termed, 'tap, trap and trace', should there not be regular and precise judicial reviews? In another sphere, internet providers are worried. Their compliance with revealing their clients' sources and contacts to an inspectorate might involve them in lawsuits.

Debatable issues, of course, abound when governments justify stern provisions as the inevitable consequence of coping with threats and emergencies. An interesting set of perspectives can be found in Amnesty International's recently-published Annual Report for 2003. Amnesty recognises that contemporary terrorism needs addressing urgently and firmly. However, security for all means human rights for all. Real security can only be achieved through full respect for human rights. Nobody should be able to pick and choose their obligations under international law. A combination of forces is seeking to roll back the human rights gains of the last five decades in the name of security and counter-terrorism. These restrictions in liberty have not necessarily led to increased dividends on safety. A more secure world, in Amnesty's view, demands a paradigm shift in the concept of security, a shift that recognises that insecurity and violence are best tackled by effective, accountable states which uphold, not violate human rights. Effective countering of terrorists depends upon knowing where to look and how to look. 'Governments are not entitled to respond to terror with terror' (*Amnesty International Report* 2003: 7–8, 10).

Amnesty's conclusion mirrors one heard constantly today, namely, that a global response to terrorism will change geopolitics as countries take sides finding their interests coalesce around a shared concern to build safety, stability and prosperity, things that terrorists and their sponsors attempt to bring to ground. There will be those who join the 'coalition of the willing', in the phrase of President George Bush, and those who stand away from it. A prominent liberal group in the United States, Human Rights Watch, is sure that some governments use a cynical strategy of touting their own internal struggles as battles against terrorists.

Russian rhetoric labels secessionists in Chechnya as terrorists, China, likewise, in provinces looking for more autonomy. Egypt is reckoned to resort to torture and trials of dissenters. Israel, Zimbabwe, Burma, Uzbekhistan and Turkey, are thought to display a knee-jerk reaction to certain radical opponents which goes beyond any human toleration. Those who are not 'with us' are terrorists.

A statement by New York-based Human Rights Watch in January 2002 makes a fitting conclusion to this chapter: 'Terrorists,' they declare,

> believe anything goes in the name of their cause. The fight against terror must not buy into that logic. It must reaffirm in principle that no civilian should ever be deliberately killed or abused. But for too many countries the anti-terrorist mantra provides new reasons for ignoring human rights.
>
> (*Guardian*, 17 January 2002)

11 Résumé and further enquiry

This chapter is in two sections. First, there is a résumé of the whole book, pointing up the most significant features in the text. There follows a set of suggestions to readers of issues that call for reflection, further discussion and enquiry.

At the outset, definition of destructive political action (using political in the widest sense) will be speculative and debatable. Beyond the basics of premeditated action, power contest, and publicity intent, there is little that can be guaranteed to stand clearly without many reservations. International bodies such as the UN and the EU have found it almost impossible to achieve consensus. To understand analytically rather than descriptively, a scrutiny of the context (historical, geographical and sociological) is essential for definition.

A second chapter worked backwards from contemporary terrorism, endemic in the Middle East, South East Asia and Central America, to earlier perspectives. Following the protest movements, as one might term them, of antiquity, of Imperial Russia, of nineteenth century Marxist contest in Europe, there has been a gathering together of resolute activists fighting for a cause but readily labelled 'terrorists' by authority. The 'freedom fighters' of the 1950s and 1960s, straining to loosen imperial shackles, were watched globally by a vast audience which either supported them or disapproved. Right and Left fought it out in Europe after 1918, the Resistance of the Second World War won both persecution and acclaim. The 1940s and 1950s brought total war and total terror in genocide. Contemporary terrorism touches every country and is multivariate in origin and style. It is distinctive historically in a widened dispersion and on a hugely escalated scale. Nobody now feels safe. Distance is no protector. There are no non-combatants.

Surveying today's scene would demand an enormous canvas. Five very different groups were chosen. The great network of al-Qaida dominated in its destructive record so far and in the world-wide threat that it poses, fuelled by politico–religious intensity. A suicidal element is the hallmark of Hizbullah, and the Tamil Tigers of Sri Lanka, though here one detected the beginnings of a move towards compromise. The last two groups, ETA in northern Spain and IRA in Ulster, have long histories of myth and memory to sustain what appears to be a losing battle to retain respect and understanding among the wearied public surrounding them. The question here is: what makes them go on with their recourse to terror?

Terrorist motivation was something that needed close examination. Once again, definition is clouded by hypothesis and anecdote with little that can be understood as confessions by terrorists. The more academic discussions of motivation attempt to isolate what can be thought of as core motives, secondary or mid-term motives and long-range goals. Once more, we need to look carefully at what appear to be causative factors that frame a context. Clearly, these can be seen as preconditions and events. It was noted that terrorists will often declare that they had no alternative, there was no other way, on account of the unreasonableness and hostility of their opposition. A concluding question here was the opportunity society may take to rehabilitate and reintegrate the terrorist 'outsider'.

Profiles of three terrorists were employed to put life into stereotypes. The depiction, in some depth, of Timothy McVeigh, Theodore Kaczynski, the 'Unabomber' and Osama bin Laden brought out the distinctiveness of contemporary terrorists. The angry young man, the disaffected mathematics professor, the tycoon-terrorist all acted out of a built-up determination to go their own way to reorder the world. There were some elements in common – dissatisfaction, a concern to defend themselves against a conspiracy (state tyranny, environmental threat, religious heresy), and an impulse to move towards something better through destruction of what was wrong in their eyes. There emerged through the three cameos the sense that these terrorists acted out of principle. A proactive component preceded anything reactive.

Strategy and tactics deserve fair attention. Tactics are generally recognisable as the purposeful and feasible steps that terrorists take to translate aims into action; strategy is the overall master-plan that lies behind them, whether its outlines are promulgated by the participants in direct action or whether it is the result of our observing and deduction. Contemporary terrorism employs a diverse repertoire of methods, many of them increasingly technical and often remote-controlled. All too clearly the terrorist–tactician leaves little to chance by way of prior reconnaissance, appraisal of resources, their own and those of a security force, mode of operation and, overall, an exercise in cost–benefit. Strategies and tactics in today's world of terror can be seen as inheriting from 'trailblazers' much that was tried out and enunciated by them, namely, low-intensity conflict, 'guided violence', and urban guer-rilla warfare. Their way was through violence (no other option) that would demonstrate political conviction. Liberation of the 'wretched of the earth' is a carefully orchestrated campaign with the liberator-in-chief as hero, never destroyer. How far, though, does the terrorist go if he believes (as most of them do) that violence begets violence? In apartheid South Africa and among Palestinians today the dilemma has shown the terrorist to be mindful rather than mindless. On the other hand, the practice of suicide bombing among fanatical groups is a tactic difficult to see as positive or rational.

Terrorists and the media is an exploratory theme of immense importance since this is the zone of contact for the majority. Image is all-important. The image exploits the imaginations of the audience. The message that pictures and recorded sound convey is unidirectional and entirely declaratory. Tuning into terrorism is for most people a theatrical experience and that is what terrorists require for immediacy and closeness of impact. Even if the media coverage of an incident avoids sensationalism, its veritable reporting is an achievement terrorists will welcome.

Are terrorists evil? This frequently heard question headed a look at ethical and moral aspects of terrorism. Consideration of the meaning usually given this term points to the moral allegiance and values-standpoint of those who habitually use it. Another issue frequently debated is the extent to which one can say that terrorists contemplating or carrying out their destructive action are disengaged morally when they depersonalise their targets and dehumanise consequences. There is reason to believe that for the intending terrorist the experience of training and of peer pressure may serve to anaesthetise inhibitory feelings and conventional codes. Also of relevance here was the mindset of those who strive to counter terrorism. Is it possible to differentiate 'moralists' from 'realists' where policies and programmes may be variously ordered and implemented according to the relationship between expediency-ruling and ethics-restraint?

Contemporary terrorism has been already perceived as moving into mega-terror and techno-terror in scale and method. Are terrorists in future years likely to avail themselves of the global availability of non-conventional weaponry, that is to say, of chemical, biological and nuclear devices? They are all mass-killers. They present risks to those who would acquire and use them. The first two are either disconcertingly easy to buy or steal, the last is almost impossible to obtain as a fully loaded explosive device but it has, instead, the awesome characteristics of radioactivity. Although chemical weapons have been used in the Tokyo underground and there are reports all the time of likely terrorists trying to acquire chemical and biological substances, the threat at present remains a hypothetical one. Given the hideousness of this particular 'risk' picture, the best precaution for the present seems to be official preparedness and a calm and informed public awareness.

Counter-terrorism was the theme of the final chapter. Principles in general use were surveyed, with the rejoinder that since there would be a good deal of disagreement among those charged with rapid and thorough counter-action a set of principles were best understood as pragmatic objectives or desirable objectives to govern programme design. The main emphasis of this chapter was on programming by the United Nations, the European Union and the governments, particularly, of Britain and the United States. There was much that was common ground in precept, planning and practice to 'neutralise' contemporary terrorism.

Unsurprisingly, the main point at issue, in considering terrorism as a worldwide menace, is what is it that is being deplored and countered? A final statement in this book is the assertion of Rosalyn Higgins, doyenne of international law, that there is no legal significance in the term 'terrorism'. It seems to be a form of shorthand to refer to activities and persons whose behaviour we find both reprehensible and threatening. Certainly, in the term and among the terrorists of today there is no universality, only unpredictability and variability. We seem to be back where we started with a search for meaning and consequently a way of coming to terms with it to make sense of our attitudes and behaviour. Perhaps that is no bad thing if it encourages us to reflect afresh, to explore possibilities and to discuss them together.

Further discussion and enquiry

This is a tentative list of points and questions that deserve further study. They are not printed in any particular order:

1 The term 'terrorism' is given the meaning we consider it deserves. Definition is 'a self-righteous, one-way, moral–legal scan of positive images of Western values which stand threatened' (Professor Richard A. Falk, Princeton University, December 2002). Is this fair comment?

2 In a democracy how far can protest be allowed to go? Stemmed, it bursts into violence.

3 Is a global 'war on terrorism' the best way of tackling 100 terrorist groups in more than 70 countries?

4 'Those who are not with us must be terrorists' (President George Bush, September 2001). What are the implications of this statement?

5 Why did the UN find it difficult generally to approve of 'freedom fighters' using violence in an armed struggle to achieve liberation?

6 A moral assertion would be that if violence leads to violence then no government is entitled to respond to terror with terror. Do you agree?

7 'Refusal to understand the roots of terrorism guarantees its perpetuation' (President Bill Clinton in London, October 2002). Does this follow?

8 ' "Homeland security" can only be totally assured at the price of paralysing open society, disrupting ordinary civilian life and abandoning civil liberties' (Rt Hon. Tony Blair, February 2003). Do we have a dilemma here?

9 Do private security organisations, as mooted in Britain and the United States, represent any sort of danger?

10 In respect of reducing Ulster's terrorism, Senator Mitchell, an American peacemaker, has said that not only arms but 'mind-sets' should be decommissioned. What could be the meaning of that?

11 Does branding terrorists as 'evil', 'barbaric' and 'fanatical', if it leads to 'never cut a deal with a terrorist', foreclose all possibility of approach and possible reconciliation?

12 How do we deal with the terrorist claim that they had no alternative than to resort to destructive violence?

13 Particularly in Northern Ireland, and also in Sri Lanka, violent action has been sustained and justified from time to time by reference to myths of invincibility, victimhood and sacrifice. How are beliefs such as these to be countered?

14 'The journalist, hungry for news and not averse to garbing it sensationally, may be the best friend of the terrorist, hungry for publicity' (*Guardian*, 14 July 2002). Is this a fair point?

15 'A catastrophic terrorist incident usually leads to widespread irrational fear and uncertainty. The terrorist triumphs' (*The Times*, 14 December 2002). What steps can a government take to reassure the public at large?

16 'George Bush's Manichean declaration of war on evil answered a need in the American public for moral clarity, spiritual consolation and recovered nerve' (Simon Schama, *Guardian*, 11 September 2002). Did it, in fact, then, help?

17 'Did the world change after 9/11? Or did America enter it – the wider world was a little closer' (*The Times*, 14 July 2002). Again, what are the implications of this?

18 'The United States is losing the battle for the world's hearts and minds while fighting terror if it turns a cold and steely eye away from millions dying of hunger and disease. Fighting poverty and under-development is part of the fight against terror' (Senator Edward Kennedy, United States, May 2003).

19 It is frequently put about by counter-terrorist personnel that if terrorists fight 'dirty' without moral qualms then why care about their rights and countering them according to conventional moral codes? The only thing that works in a dire situation is a 'dead or alive' policy. Too many principles hamper a swift and sure settlement of a terrorist scenario. Does this suggest a 'realist' perspective rather than a 'moral' one? Are these positions irreconcilable?

20 'It is worth exploring defeating terrorists by dialogue as well as intelligence and military action' (Rt Hon. David Owen, January 2003). What possibilities might there ever be?

An outline typology

A final suggestion that some readers might find useful is to study the typology printed below. Richard Schultz (1978) developed a useful outline framework of political terrorism that is summarised here and illustrated in an accompanying table. There are three generalised categories of political action by internal or external agents:

1   Revolutionary terrorism – the threat or use of political violence aimed at effecting complete revolutionary change.
2   Sub-revolutionary terrorism – the threat or use of political violence aimed at effecting various changes in a particular political system (but not to abolish it).
3   Establishment terrorism – the threat or use of political violence by an established political system against internal or external opposition.

There are seven possible variables:

1   Causes – any one or more of observable economic, political, social, psychological factors (long-term or short-term) under-lying a decision to use violence.
2   Environment – (internal) urban/rural movements within the nation state; (external) global, other nation states.
3   Goals – objectives as long-range plans or as short-term tactics.
4   Strategy – overall plan with necessary policies, actions and instruments.
5   Means – capabilities and techniques varying in destructive effort, cost, practicality and frequency of use, propaganda.
6   Organisation – structure, leadership, delegation, specific responsibilities, training, recruitment, logistic support, intelligence, funding.
7   Participation – committed activists, full-time and part-time members, passive sympathisers.

The Schultz typology is presented as Table 1.

Table 1 Typology of political terrorism

Selected variables	Causes	Environment	Goals	Strategy	Means	Organisation	Participation
General categories							
Revolutionary terrorism	Economic, political, social, psychological factors	Internal (urban or rural revolutionary groups)	Long-range/ strategic objectives	Primary or secondary role in the overall strategy	Various capabilities and techniques employed	Nature – degrees of organisational structures	Participant profiles
		External (autono- mous non-state revolutionary actors)	Short-term/ tactical objectives				Leadership style/attitude
Sub-revolutionary terrorism	Economic, political, social, psychological factors	Internal (urban or rural non- revolutionary groups)	Long-range/ strategic objectives	Primary or secondary role in the overall strategy	Various capabilities and techniques employed	Nature – degrees of organisational structures	Participant profiles
		External (non- revolutionary, autonomous, non-state actors)	Short-term/ tactical objectives				Leadership style/attitude
Establishment terrorism	Economic, political, social, psychological factors	Internal (repression of urban or rural opposition)	Long-range/ strategic objectives strategy	Primary or secondary role in the overall strategy	Various capabilities and techniques employed	Nature – degrees of organisational structures	Participant profiles
		External (aimed at other nation-states or non-state actors)	Short-term/ tactical objectives				Leadership style/attitude

Source: Whittaker 2003: 34

Any typology should be labelled 'use with care'. All too easily one may be led along deterministic paths. It is the variables that are likely to provoke most controversy. Many factors may be considered 'observable' but, of course, they will be subject to the vagaries of observers' judgements. In this typology the variable 'environment' should be understood as the *context* (internal or external) within which terrorists operate – a concept, we have noted, much stressed by Crenshaw (1995). Goals or objectives, as Chapter 6 pointed out, will be strategic or tactical within longer or shorter time-frames. They may not always be clearly distinguishable as they are proclaimed on terrorist agendas or as the conclusions of observers. Organisational variables will encompass terrorist groups that are large-scale, small-scale, horizontally dispersed or pyramidical with a hierarchy. Again, as we have seen, terrorist activity may be long-lasting or episodic. Some groups feature dominant leaders and supervisory elites while others depend for cohesion on top-down control and willing participants in a task force.

The Schultz scheme is tentatively offered as a yardstick to readers grappling with the wide range of issues that this book has already introduced. Worth remembering, perhaps, is Crenshaw's point (Crenshaw 1995: 5) that: 'the causal claim that leads to the commission of acts of terrorism is complex. It can be pictured as a narrowing funnel, a last stage of which is the decision to commit an act of terrorism'.

Appendix I
Where to find out more

Introductory books

Two of my earlier books will be useful introductions to a very complex field of study:

The Terrorism Reader (2nd edn 2003), London: Routledge, is a carefully assembled, edited selection of the views of a number of well-known authorities on political violence. Among other things, it illustrates the growth and variety of terrorism with a series of 13 contrasted case-studies from four continents. There is a substantial list of references as a guide to further reading and notes on further sources of information.

Terrorism: Understanding the Global Threat (2002), London: Pearson/Longman, is a less-academic, plain-purposed survey of terrorism written to inform readers and help them understand the nature of terrorism.

Other introductory books

Crenshaw, Martha (ed.) (1995), *Terrorism in Context*, Pennsylvania State University Press.
An interdisciplinary set of essays; wide-ranging, detailed, illuminating.
Hoffman, Bruce (1999), *Inside Terrorism*, London: Indigo.
An excellent starter. Fresh, comprehensive approach.
Laqueur, Walter (1999), *The New Terrorism*, London: Oxford University Press.

Panoramic, lively study. Extensive, up-to-date bibliography. Indispensable.

Reich, Walter (1998), *Origins of Terrorism*, London: John Hopkins University Press.

'Honest, penetrating effort to explain the role of human psychology in terrorism' *Canadian Journal of Political Science* (quoted on back cover). Most useful.

Saad-Ghorayeb, Amal (2001), *Hizbu'llah: Politics and Religion*, London: Pluto.

Highly informative. An eye-opener on Middle Eastern affairs generally.

Schmid, A. P. and Crelinstein, R. D. (eds) (1993), *Western Responses to Terrorism*, London: Cassell.

Original in thought, explores issues widely.

Other references in the text

Amnesty International Report (2003), London: Amnesty International Publications.

Bodansky, Yossef (2001), *Bin Laden: the Man who Declared War on America*, California: Prima Publicity.

CNN News (1997), Online. Available www.cnn.com/SPECIALS/1997/unabomb.htm (accessed May 2003).

Crenshaw, Martha (1981), 'The causes of terrorism', *Comparative Politics*, July 1981: 381–5.

European Union (2003), Online. Available www.europa.eu.int/com/110901.htm (accessed May 2003).

Gillespie, Richard (1982), *Soldiers of Peron, Argentina's Montoneros*, Oxford: Oxford University Press.

Huntington, Samuel P. (1996), *The Clash of Civilisations and the Remaking of World Order*, New York: Simon and Schuster.

Huntington, Samuel P. (2002), 'Muslim wars', *Newsweek Special Issue*, November 2002, 9–13, New York: Newsweek Publications.

International Policy Institute for Counter-terrorism (December 2001), Online. Available www.ict.org.il/articles December 2001.htm (accessed June 2003).

International Policy Institute for Counter-terrorism (2003), Online. Available www.ict.org.il/bin Laden.htm (accessed April 2003).

Khatchadourian, Haig (1998), *The Morality of Terrorism*, New York: Peter Lang.

Mandela, Nelson (1997), *Long Walk to Freedom*, London: Abacus.

Miller, Judith (2001), *Germs, Biological Weapons and America's Second War*, New York: Simon and Schuster.

Mitchell, G. (1997), *Mitchell Report*, Belfast: Northern Ireland Government Office. Online. Available www.nio.gov.uk/agreement.htm (accessed July 2003).

The Record (6 December 2001), Online. Available www.therecord.com/news 6 December 2001.htm (accessed May 2003).

Said, Edward, 'The myth of the clash of civilisations', lecture on videocassette, Northampton Massachusetts Media Education Foundation, 1998.

Schultz, Richard (1978), 'Conceptualizing political terrorism', *Journal of International Affairs*, vol. 32, no. 1, Spring/Summer 1978.

Seto, Theodore P. (2002), 'The morality of terrorism. Report of seminar Terrorism and the Law', Loyola Law School, *Loyola of Los Angeles Law Review*, vol. 35, no. 4.

Shaw, Martin (2001), 'A regressive crystallization of global state power: theorising a response to the "war against terrorism"'. Online. Available www.theglobalsite.ac.uk/press/109shaw.htm (accessed July 2003).

Shaw, Martin (2002), 'Ten challenges to anti-war politics'. Online. Available www.theglobalsite.ac.uk/justpeace/111shaw.htm (accessed July 2003).

United Nations (November 2001), Online. Available www.un.org/News/dh/latest/feature-terror-disarm.htm (accessed April 2003).

Washington Post (2 July 1995), Online. Available www.dir.yahoo.com/Oklahoma City/Timothy McVeigh Case.htm (accessed May 2003).

Williams, Paul L. (2002), *Al Qaeda Brotherhood of Terror*, New York: Alpha Pearson.

Newspapers and magazines referred to in the text

Belfast Telegraph (26 April 1996)

Guardian (10 April 2001, 12 October 2001, 17 January 2002, 14 July 2002)

Herald Tribune (25 February 2003)

New York Times (21 December 2001)

Northern Echo (30 December 2002)

Pakistan Daily News (19 June 2001)
The Record (6 December 2001)
The Times (23 October 1997, 14 July 2002, 14 December 2002)
Time Magazine (December 1998)
Washington Post (15 October 2001)

Journals

From time to time, articles of relevant interest appear in:

Foreign Affairs
International Affairs
International Relations
International Studies
Millennium Review of International Studies
Political Science Quarterly
Studies in Conflict and Terrorism
Terrorism and Political Violence

Useful addresses

Centre for the Study of Political Violence, Department of International Relations, University of St Andrews, St Andrews, Fife KY16 9AJ.
UK Islamic Mission, 202 North Gower Street, London NW1 2LY.
United Nations Department of Public Information, Public Enquiries Unit, UN Plaza, New York NY 10017, United States.

Apart from printed material readily available from the above, these international websites will yield a great deal of information:

British Library (UK) OPAC 97 Service http//opac97.bl.uk
Center for Defense and International Security Studies www.cdiss. org.hometemp.htm
International Policy Institute for Counter-terrorism (Israel) www. ict.org.il
Israeli Government Press Office www.gpo.gov.il
Jane's Information Group www.janes.com
Terrorism Research Center (USA) www.terrorism.com
United Nations www.un.org

US State Department Office of Counter-terrorism www.state.gov/
www/global/terrorism/index.htm

It is worthwhile putting keywords to a reliable search engine, e.g.
terrorism, counter-terrorism, ETA, Che Guevara, IRA, guerrilla
warfare, Osama bin Laden, World Trade Center, etc.

Appendix II
Contemporary terrorist groups

It is not easy to compile a list of terrorist groups active today. The tally worldwide is never a static one. There are high-profile organisations with dynamic leaders and consistent strategies. Many of these groups have been active for many years and the counter-terrorist organisations know them well. There are a number of small groups with shifts in management, motives, political action and numbers. Their aims and intentions may be difficult to discern. This list (derived in the main from press sources) is far from comprehensive but it does indicate that contemporary terrorism is both far-flung and diverse. This list names organisations and national locales or affiliations.

Organisation	National affiliation
Abu Sayyaf Group (ASG)	Philippines
Ansar al-Islam	Kurds, Northern Iraq
Al-Aqsa Martyrs Brigade	Palestine
Armata Corsa	France
Armed Islamic Group (GIA)	Algeria
Armenian Secret Army for Liberation	Armenia
Aum Shinrikyo	Japan
Baluch People's Liberation Front	Northern India
Basque Homeland and Freedom (ETA)	Spain
Chechen Rebels	Chechnya
Chukaku-Ha (Nucleus or Middle Core Faction)	Japan
Continuity Irish Republican Army	Northern Ireland

Democratic Front for the Liberation of Palestine (DFLP)	Palestine
Direct Action (Action Directe)	France
Fatah – Revolutionary Council (Abu Nidal Organisation)	Lebanon
Fatah Tanzim	Palestine
Force 17	Palestine
Free Papua Movement	Papua
Al-Gama'a al-Islamiyya (The Islamic Group, IG)	Egypt
Hamas (Islamic Resistance Movement)	Palestine
Harakat ul-Mujahidin (HUM)	Pakistan
Hizbullah (Party of God)	Lebanon
Hizb-ul Mujahidin	Pakistan
Irish National Liberation Army	Northern Ireland
Irish Republican Army (IRA)	Northern Ireland
Islamic Movement of Uzbekistan	Uzbekistan
Jamaat ul-Fuqra	Pakistan
Jammu and Kashmir National Liberation Army	Northern India
Japanese Red Army (JRA)	Japan
Jemaah Islamiya	Malaysia
Jihad Group	Egypt
Kach and Kahane Chai	Israel
Kumpulan Mujahidin Malaysia	Malaysia
Kurdistan Worker's Party (PKK)	Turkey
Lashkar-e-Toiba	Pakistan
Lautaro Youth Movement (MJL)	Chile
Lebanese Armed Revolutionary Faction	Lebanon
Liberation Tigers of Tamil Eelam (LTTE)	Sri Lanka
Loyalist Volunteer Force (LVF)	Northern Ireland
Manuel Rodriquez Patriotic Front (FPMR)	Chile
Martyrs of al-Aqsa	Palestine
Al-Maunah Islamic Group	Malaysia
Moranzanist Patriotic Front (FPM)	Honduras
Moro Islamic Liberation Front (MILF)	Philippines

Movement for the Jordanian Islamic Resistance	Jordan
Mujahidin-e Khalq Organisation (MEK or MKO)	Iran
National Liberation Army (ELN) Colombia	Colombia
National Liberation Front of Corsica (FLNC)	France
National Union for the Total Independence of Angola (UNITA)	Angola
Nestor Paz Zamora Commission (CNPZ)	Bolivia
New People's Army (NPA)	Philippines
Palestine Liberation Front (PLF)	Iraq
Palestinian Islamic Jihad (PIJ)	Palestine
Party of Democratic Kampuchea (Khmer Rouge)	Cambodia
Patriotic Committee for Venezuela	Venezuela
Pattari United Liberation Army	Thailand
Popular Front for the Liberation of Palestine – General Command	Palestine
Popular Front for the Liberation of Palestine (PFLP)	Palestine
Popular Liberation Army	Ecuador
Popular Struggle Front (PSF)	Syria
Provisional Irish Republican Army ('Provos')	Northern Ireland
Al-Qaida (the Base)	Afghanistan
Qibla and People Against Gangsterism and Drugs (PAGAD)	South Africa
Real IRA	Northern Ireland
Red Army Faction (RAF)	Germany
Red Brigades (BR)	Italy
Revolutionary Armed Forces of Colombia (FARC)	Colombia
Revolutionary Organisation 17 November	Greece
Revolutionary People's Liberation Party/ Front (DHCP/F)	Turkey
Revolutionary People's Struggle (ELA)	Greece
Sendero Luminoso (Shining Path)	Peru
Sipah-e-Sahaba Pakistan (SSP)	Pakistan
Sudan People's Liberation Army	Sudan

Tupac Amaru Revolutionary Movement (MRTA)	Peru
United Forces of Caucasian Mujahidin	Caucasus
United Self-Defence Forces of Colombia	Colombia
Xinjiang (Muslim Group)	China

Appendix III
Chronology of terrorist incidents
1968–2003

This list of notable terrorist incidents between 1968 and the present can only be a selection to give some idea of the frequency, nature and location of incidents. Much of the data has been culled from press sources.

1968   Mid-air hijacking of Rome–Tel Aviv plane by three Palestinians. Passengers to be exchanged for Palestinians in Israeli prisons.

1968   London – Young Angry Brigade members let off 25 bombs over next three years.

1970   Jordan – four planes hijacked by Palestinians. One goes to Cairo, the other three are destroyed on return to Jordan.

1971   Uruguay – British ambassador kidnapped and held for eight months by Tupamoros terrorists.

1972   Belfast – IRA bomb attack kills 11, injures 130. British army reprisal known as 'Bloody Sunday'.

1972   Munich – eight Palestinian terrorists (Black September) take Israeli Olympic athletes hostage in exchange for 236 Palestinians. Bungled German rescue kills five terrorists and all nine hostages.

1972   Israel – Japanese terrorists (acting for Palestinians) kill 26 at airport, injure nine.

1973   Sudan – US ambassador and staff killed by Black September group.

1974   Paris – Japanese terrorists bomb discotheque, killing two, injuring five.

1975   New York – Puerto Rican nationalists bomb Wall Street bar, four die, 60 injured.

1976   Uganda – Air France plane seized by Baader-Meinhof gunmen, forced to land. Israeli commandos rescue passengers.

1978   Rome – Premier Aldo Moro kidnapped by Red Brigade, killed after two months.

1979   Teheran – US embassy staff taken hostage by Islamic students. President Carter orders abortive rescue. Eventual release after two months.

1979   Ireland – IRA kill Lord Mountbatten by bombing his fishing boat.

1980   Bologna – Right wing group bomb station, killing 84, injuring 180.

1980   Munich – Right wing group bomb Oktoberfest, killing 14, injuring 215.

1981   Ramstein, West Germany – Red Army explode bomb at US Air Force base. No casualties.

1982   London – IRA car bomb decimates troop of mounted Lifeguards.

1983   Beirut – Islamic Jihad suicide car bomb, at US and French barracks. 300 die.

1983   Beirut – US embassy hit by truck bomb. Islamic Jihad responsible. 63 die, 120 injured.

1984   India – Sikh terrorists seize Amritsar's Golden Temple. Rescuing kills 100.

1984   Lebanon – Terry Waite, Archbishop of Canterbury's envoy, abducted until 1992.

1984   Torrejon, Spain – Hizbullah bomb restaurant near US base. 18 die, 83 injured.

1984   Brighton – IRA bomb fails to kill Prime Minister Thatcher and Cabinet at conference.

1985   Beirut, Algiers – Rome–Cairo plane hijacked by Hizbullah and flown to Beirut, to Algiers and back to Beirut. Intense diplomatic efforts to secure release of passengers and crew. Hostages held in Beirut until President Reagan yields.

1985   East Mediterranean – Palestinians seize Italian cruise liner *Achille Lauro*, taking 700 hostages. One dies. Egypt offers terrorists sanctuary in return for passengers' release.

1986   West Berlin – Libyan bomb attack on café popular with GIs. 81 casualties. US military jets retaliate by strafing Tripoli, Quaddafi's capital.

1987   Athens – bus bombing by 17 November organisation. 16 US servicemen injured.

1988   Lockerbie, Scotland – in-flight bombing of Pan Am plane by Libyans. 259 passengers and 11 on the ground die.

1989   Chad – in-flight bombing of French plane by Islamic *Jihad*, killing 171.

1991   London – IRA mortar attack on Cabinet Meeting at Downing Street fails.

1992   Buenos Aires – Israeli embassy bombed by Hizbullah. 29 die, 242 injured.

1993   New York – World Trade Center. Sunni group attempt destruction with bomb and gas cloud. Partial failure but 11 die, many injured.

1993   Bombay – Islamic group car bomb kills 400, injures 1,000.

1993   Colombia – Revolutionary Armed Forces of Colombia kidnap three US missionaries. Ransom eventually paid.

1994   West Bank, Israel – Jewish right wing extremist machine-guns Muslims at prayer, killing 29, wounding 150.

1995   London – IRA bomb Canary Wharf, injuring thousands.

1995   Tokyo – nerve gas attack by Aum Shinrikyo cult, on subway. 12 die, 5,000 injured.

1995   Oklahoma City – Timothy McVeigh bombs downtown office complex.

1995   United States – 'Unabomber' mails home-made bombs and blackmails the press. Arrested.

1995   Nairobi, Dar es-Salaam – al-Qaida car bombs US embassies. 224 die, 5,000 injured.

1996   Cairo – Islamic terrorist machine-guns foreign tourists, killing 18.

1996   Peru – Japanese terrorists abduct guests at Japanese ambassador's party. Negotiated end.

1996   Manchester – IRA severely damages city centre, injuring many.

1996   Colombo – Tamil Tigers ram bank with bomb-laden truck. 90 die, 1,400 injured.

1997   Egypt – Islamic terrorists kill 58 foreigners at Luxor's temple.

1997   New York – Palestinian gunman shoots three tourists at Empire State Building.

1997   Jerusalem – Hamas suicide bombers bomb shops, killing eight, injuring 200.

1998   Ulster – IRA bomb in Omagh kills 29, injures 330, despite ceasefire.

1998   Colombia – National Liberation Army bomb pipeline. 71 die, 100 injured.

2000   Yemen – al-Qaida bombs USS *Cole*, killing 17, wounding 40.

2001   New York, Washington – two hijacked planes demolish World Trade Center twin towers. Pentagon bombed. One other plane misses, perhaps White House target, crashes in Pennsylvania. Worst ever disaster – nearly 3,000 die. US builds ambitious anti-terrorist programme, and forms a global coalition against terrorism.

2001   United States – United States and other countries have suspect anthrax spores in mail. Some deaths, hoaxes abound. Tests, investigations, point to disgruntled US scientist as source.

2001   Tel Aviv – Hamas bomb nightclub, injuring 140.

2001   Jerusalem, Haifa – Palestinians use car bombs; savage Israeli retaliation.

2002   Philippines – nail bomb kills three, leads to great panic.

2002   Bali – al-Qaida bombs nightclub. 187 die, 300 injured, many of them tourists.

2002   Kuwait – shooting of US soldiers on training exercise; suicide bombing of French army base.

2002   Manila – Abu Sayyaf Islamic group bomb shops. Five die, 100 injured.

2002   Moscow – Chechen terrorists, 50 of them, take 700 hostages in a theatre audience. Rescue attempt kills all the Chechens but gas used in storming the building kills 90 of the hostages.

2002   Kashmir – Islamic militants shoot into bazaar crowd. 13 die, 50 injured.

2002   Jerusalem – Hamas suicide bomber kills 11 and injures 50.

2002   Mombasa, Kenya – al-Qaida bomb hotel. 13 die, 80 injured, many of them tourists.

2002   West Bank mortar attack by Hamas partly averted by security forces, 10 injured.

2002 Chechnya – Russian army bus bombed by Chechens, killing 15.

2003 Belfast – Real IRA time-set truck bomb defused just in time.

2003 Sri Lanka – Tamil Tigers strafe and sink Chinese fishing boat, 18 die.

2003 Saudi Arabia – al-Qaida suicide bomb left in US housing complex, killing 29, injuring 160.

2003 Groznym, Chechnya – Chechens mine a Russian army bus, three die, eight injured.

2003 Jerusalem – Hamas bomb a bus, killing 15, injuring 50.

Index